THE DOOL
RAID

THE DOOLITTLE RAID

THE FIRST AIR ATTACK AGAINST JAPAN, APRIL 1942

JOHN GREHAN

and

ALEXANDER NICOLL

AIR WORLD

AIR WORLD

THE DOOLITTLE RAID
The First Air Attack Against Japan, April 1942

First published in Great Britain in 2020 by Air World Books,
an imprint of Pen & Sword Books Ltd,
Yorkshire – Philadelphia

Typeset in 9.5/12.5 avenir by Dave Cassan

Printed and bound in the UK by CPI Group (UK) Ltd, Croydon, CR0 4YY

Pen & Sword Books Ltd incorporates the imprints of Air World Books, Pen & Sword Archaeology, Atlas, Aviation, Battleground, Discovery, Family History, History, Maritime, Military, Naval, Politics, Social History, Transport, True Crime, Claymore Press, Frontline Books, Praetorian Press, Seaforth Publishing and White Owl

For a complete list of Pen & Sword titles please contact:

PEN & SWORD BOOKS LTD
47 Church Street, Barnsley, South Yorkshire, S70 2AS, UK.
E-mail: enquiries@pen-and-sword.co.uk
Website: www.pen-and-sword.co.uk

Or

PEN AND SWORD BOOKS,
1950 Lawrence Roadd, Havertown, PA 19083, USA
E-mail: Uspen-and-sword@casematepublishers.com
Website: www.penandswordbooks.com

CONTENTS

Acknowledgements   vi

Part I

STRIKING BACK

Chapter 1   Introduction   1
Chapter 2   Making it Happen   8
Chapter 3   All At Sea   14

Part II

TARGET JAPAN

Saturday, 18 April 1942   47

Crew 1   Lieutenant Colonel Doolittle, B-25 Mitchell #40-2344   65
Crew 2   Lieutenant Travis Hoover, B-25 Mitchell #40-2292   71
Crew 3   Lieutenant Robert M. Gray, B-25 Mitchell #40-2270   74
Crew 4   Lieutenant Everett W. Holstrom, B-25 Mitchell #40-2282   77
Crew 5   Captain David M. Jones, B-25 Mitchell #40-2283   79
Crew 6   Lieutenant Dean E. Hallmark, B-25 Mitchell #40-2298   82
Crew 7   Lieutenant Ted W. Lawson, B-25 Mitchell #40-2261   85
Crew 8   Captain Edward J. York, B-25 Mitchell #40-2242   88
Crew 9   Lieutenant Harold F. Watson, B-25 Mitchell #40-2303   90
Crew 10   Lieutenant Richard O. Joyce, B-25 Mitchell #40-2250   93
Crew 11   Captain Charles Ross Greening, B-25 Mitchell #40-2249   96
Crew 12   Lieutenant William M. Bower, B-25 Mitchell #40-2278   98
Crew 13   Lieutenant Edgar E. McElroy, B-25 Mitchell #40-2247   100
Crew 14   Major John A. Hilger, B-25 Mitchell #40-2297   105
Crew 15   Lieutenant Donald G. Smith, B-25 Mitchell #40-2267   111
Crew 16   Lieutenant William G. Farrow, B-25 Mitchell #40-2268   113

Part III

THE AFTERMATH

Chapter 4   War Crimes   121
Chapter 5   The Post-Raid Assessment   123
Chapter 6   Recreating History   160

References and Notes   176

ACKNOWLEDGEMENTS

The author and publisher would like to extend their grateful thanks, in no particular order, to the following individuals and organisations for their assistance with the images used in this publication: Robert Mitchell, James Luto, Historic Military Press, US Naval History and Heritage Command, US National Museum of Naval Aviation, US National Archives and Records Administration, National Museum of the US Air Force, United States Air Force, US Navy, US Library of Congress, US Army, and the US Air Force Historical Support Division.

PART ONE

Striking Back

CHAPTER 1

Introduction

Nothing, it seemed, could stop the Japanese. Pearl Harbor had only been the beginning. Thailand, Penang, Hong Kong, Guam, Wake Island, Burma, the Dutch East Indies, New Guinea, the Solomon Islands, Manila, Kuala Lumpur and Rabaul had all fallen to the forces of Emperor Hirohito. By the middle of February 1942, Singapore, Great Britain's fortress in the East, was in Japanese hands. But the United States was already planning the fight back.

At the darkest time of the war, with Allied morale at its lowest ebb and the Japanese still advancing westwards, President Franklin D. Roosevelt called for an immediate strike upon Tokyo. There were even offers of large rewards of cash from private individuals for the first men to bomb the city. But the Japanese Imperial capital is more than 5,000 miles from the US mainland, well beyond the range of any aircraft. There appeared to be little hope of mounting a raid upon Japan any time soon. Yet already, in the utmost secrecy, just such a raid was being carefully planned.

On 10 February 1942, US Navy Captain Francis Low, Assistant Chief of Staff for anti-submarine warfare, suggested that large aircraft could be launched from carriers to strike at Japan. The normal naval carrier-borne aircraft lacked both the range and bomb-carrying capacity to achieve this, but Low believed that the United States Army Air Force's (USAAF) new twin-engine North American B-25B Mitchell bombers could be launched from an aircraft carrier. The range of the Mitchell with a full bomb load, however, was just 1,300 miles. Yet, if the aircraft were stripped of all of its non-essential equipment, including much of its defensive armament, and its bomb load reduced, the B-25's range could be considerably increased. Maybe, just maybe, one of the most audacious and ambitious air raids in history was possible.

Captain Lowe presented his idea to Admiral Ernest J. King, Commander in Chief of the United States Fleet, who immediately seized upon the scheme. Under the subject heading, 'B25B Special Project', King duly wrote to the Chief of the Army Air Forces, General Henry Harley 'Hap' Arnold:

'The purpose of this special project is to bomb and fire the industrial centers of Japan. It is anticipated that this will not only cause confusion and impede production but will undoubtedly facilitate operations against Japan in other theatres due to their probable withdrawal of troops for the purpose of defending the home country. An action of this kind is most desirable now due to the psychological effect on the American public, our allies and our enemies.

'The method contemplated is to bring carrier borne bombers to within 400 or 500 miles of the coast of Japan, preferably to the south-southeast. They will then take off from the carrier deck and proceed directly to selected objectives. These objectives will be military and industrial targets in the Tokyo-Yokohama, Nagoya and Osaka-Kobi areas.

'Simultaneous bombings of these areas is contemplated with the bombers coming in up waterways from the southeast and, after dropping their bombs, returning in the same direction ... Due to the greater accuracy of daylite [sic] bombing a daylite raid is contemplated. The present concept of the project calls for a nite [sic] take-off from the carrier and arrival over objectives at dawn …

'A nite raid will be made if due to last minute information received from our intelligence section or other source a daylite raid is definitely inadvisable. The nite raid should be made on a clear nite, moonlite [sic] if Japan is blacked out, moonless if it is not.'[1]

Naturally, General Arnold was willing to explore this seemingly impossible proposal further, as was the man he felt should lead the mission, Lieutenant Colonel James H. 'Jimmy' Doolittle. One of the world's foremost aviators, Doolittle had been a test pilot, dare-devil racer and now Arnold needed him as a trouble-shooter and project officer. 'The object of the project', Doolittle later wrote, 'was to bomb the industrial centres of Japan. It was hoped that the damage done would be both material and psychological. Material damage was to the destruction of specific targets with ensuing confusion and retardation of production. The psychological results, it was hoped, would be the recalling of combat equipment from other theaters for home defense, thus effecting relief in those theaters, the development of a fear complex in Japan, improved relationships with our allies and a favorable reaction on the American people.'[2]

There were, though, immense obstacles to overcome. Chief among these were the vast distances involved and the dominating presence across the Pacific of the hitherto victorious Japanese fleet.

The original plan was to take-off from and return to an aircraft carrier. The first objective then, before any other elements of the scheme could be considered, was to see if Captain Lowe's idea was practicable. Take-off and landing tests were duly conducted with three B-25Bs at and off Norfolk, Virginia. These tests indicated that take-off from the carrier would be relatively easy but landing back on a ship subject to unpredictable wind and waves was extremely difficult and too hazardous to be attempted. Somewhere would have to be found where the bombers could land after the raid.

After some consideration, it was decided that a carrier take-off would be made some point east of Tokyo and the flight would proceed in a generally westerly direction from there. Fields near the east coast of China, which was not under Japanese control, and at Vladivostok in the Soviet Union, were identified as the bombers' destinations. The planes would then be handed over to the Chinese Government. The principal advantage of Vladivostok as a landing point was that it was only about 600 miles from Tokyo against some 1,200 miles to the China coast – and range was the most critical factor. Surprisingly, though the US and the USSR were allies, so too were Japan and the Soviet Union, and when approached about the proposed raid, the men in power in Moscow expressed reluctance in allowing American military aircraft to land on their territory for fear of damaging relations with the Japanese. The idea of going to Vladivostok was therefore abandoned.

While the Chinese would have to be warned of the arrival of the bombers, great care had to be taken to avoid such information falling into the hands of the Japanese. A cover story was therefore prepared. The Chinese would be informed that the aircraft would be flying up from the south in order to stage a raid on Japan from which they plan to return to the same bases. Radio signals from the bombing planes immediately after they dropped could be used to advise the Chinese that the Mitchells would arrive at the refuelling points some six or seven hours later.

Opposite page: A First World War veteran, it was Captain Francis Stuart Low, pictured here in April 1943, who is credited with the idea that twin-engine bombers could be launched from an aircraft carrier. It is stated that he made this observation after watching such aircraft at a naval air station in Virginia, where the runway had been painted with the outline of an aircraft carrier deck for landing practice. (USNHHC)

Range, therefore, became of even greater importance. A distance of 2,400 miles with a bomb load of 2,000lbs was set as the aircraft requirement for the raid, and a study of the various aircraft available for this project indicated that the B-25B was, as expected, the type best suited to the purpose.

For the B-25Bs to stand any chance of reaching Tokyo extensive modifications were required. Additional fuel tanks would have to be installed and every piece of non-essential equipment removed. This work was to be carried out on twenty-four aircraft. Firstly, a steel gasoline tank of about 265-gallon capacity was manufactured by the McQuay Company and installed by the Mid-Continent Airlines at Minneapolis. This tank was later removed and replaced by a 225-gallon leak-proof tank manufactured by the United States Rubber Company at Mishawaka, Indiana. Considerable difficulty was experienced with this rubber leak-proof tank due to leaks in the connections, as well as the fact that after having made one fairly satisfactory tank, the outer case was reduced in size in order to facilitate installation without reducing the size of the inner rubber container and consequently wrinkles developed reducing the capacity and increasing the tendency to failure and leakage. Putting air pressure on the tank increased the capacity about ten to fifteen gallons and new outer covers eventually alleviated the problem. It was, however, not possible for the manufacturer to provide new covers for all of the tanks before the operation was due to be mounted, and one serious tank failure occurred the day before take-off. This was a leak caused by a failure of the inner liner resulting from sharp wrinkles which in turn were caused by the inner liner being too large and the outer case too small.

The space taken up by this additional fuel tank still left enough room in the bomb bay to permit the carrying of four 500lb demolition bombs or four 500lb incendiary clusters. It was necessary, in order to carry the bomb load, to utilise extension shackles which were also provided by the McQuay Company. The crawl way above the bomb bay was lined and a rubber bag tank, manufactured by the US Rubber Company, and holding about 160 gallons, was installed. The vent for this tank, when turned forward provided pressure and forced the gasoline out of the tank. When turned aft the vent sucked the air and vapor out of the tank and permitted it to be collapsed (after the gasoline was used) and pushed to one side. After this was done the aircraft was again completely operational as crew members could move forward or aft through the crawl way. Collapsing the tank, sucking out the vapour, and pushing it over to one side minimized the fire hazard. A very considerable amount of trouble was encountered with this tank due to leaks developing in the seams. This trouble was reduced through the use of a heavier material and more careful handling of the tank.

The third tank was a 60-gallon leak-proof tank installed in the place from which the lower turret was removed. This tank was a regular 2 feet x 2 feet x 2 feet test cell with a filler neck, outlet and vent provided. The filler neck of this rear tank was readily available in flight. Ten 5-gallon cans of gasoline were carried in the rear compartment, where the radio operator ordinarily sat, and were poured into this rear tank as the gasoline level went down. These cans later had holes punched in them so that they would sink and were thrown overboard.

Opposite page: James H. Doolittle pictured before the Second World War. Having gained his regular commission and promotion to first lieutenant in July 1920, it was in September 1922 that Doolittle had made the first of his many pioneering flights. On this occasion he flew a DH-4, equipped with crude navigational instruments, in the first cross-country flight over America, from Pablo Beach, Florida, to San Diego, California. This was achieved in a time of twenty-one hours and nineteen minutes. Doolittle made only one refuelling stop at Kelly Field. He was awarded the Distinguished Flying Cross for this historic feat. (NARA)

These measures gave each aircraft a total gallonage of 646 gallons in the main tank, 225 gallons in the bomb bay tank, 160 gallons in the crawl way tank, 60 gallons in the rear turret tank, and 50 gallons in 5-gallon tins, or 1,141 gallons, some 1,100 gallons of which were available. It would not be possible for all of the gasoline to be drained from the tanks and that during the filling operation extreme care had to be taken in order to ensure that all air was driven out and they were completely full. This could only be accomplished by filling, shaking the aircraft up and down and topping off again. The extra tanks and tank supports were designed by and installed under the supervision of the Materiel Division of the Army Air Forces.

The B-25B's fuel capacity had almost been doubled through these measures and it meant that the requirement for the bombers to achieve a range of 2,400 miles had almost been met. But more had to be done and efforts were turned towards reducing the weight of the aircraft.

The B-25's twin rear guns were removed and replaced by two wooden mock .50 calibre guns, which were stuck out of the extreme tip of the tail. The effectiveness of this subterfuge was indicated by the fact that none of the aircraft on the raid was attacked from directly behind. The lateral attacks were more difficult for the attacker and gave the machine-gunners a better target.

De-icers and anti-icers were installed on all the aircraft. Although these had the effect of slightly reducing the cruising speed, they were necessary for insurance and also because it was not decided until shortly before leaving on the mission, with negotiations with the Kremlin still ongoing, whether Vladivostok or eastern China was to be the final destination. Should it be the latter, no ice was to be expected at lower altitudes but icing conditions would be prevalent along the northern route to Vladivostok.

This measure obviously had a small impact on the B-25's range so, inasmuch as it was decided that all bombing would be done from low altitudes and as the existing Norden bomb sight did not particularly lend itself to extremely low altitude bombing, the bomb-sight was removed. A simplified sight designed by Captain C.R. Greening was installed in its place. Actual low altitude bombing tests carried out at 1,500 feet showed a greater degree of accuracy with this simplified sight than the men were able to obtain with the Norden. This not only permitted greater bombing accuracy but obviated the possibility of the Norden sight falling into enemy hands.

Pyrotechnics were removed from the Mitchells in order to reduce the fire hazard and also for the slight saving in weight. Two conventional landing flares were installed immediately forward of the rear armoured bulkhead. There was no dropping mechanism for the landing flares. It was planned, if it became necessary to use them, that they be thrown out by the rear gunner. A lanyard attached to the parachute flare and the fuselage would remove the case some six feet from the plane.

As it was planned to maintain radio silence throughout the flight, the 230lb Liaison radio set was removed.

The lead aircraft and each of the flight leaders' aircraft were equipped with electrically operated automatic cameras which took sixty pictures at one-half second intervals. The cameras could be turned on at any time by the pilot and were automatically started when the first bomb dropped. Cameras were located in the extreme tip of the tail between the two wooden .50 calibre guns. The lens angle was 35 degrees. The other ten B-25s carried 16mm movie cameras similarly mounted.

Special 500lb demolition bombs were provided. These were loaded with an explosive mixture containing 50 per cent T.N.T. and 50 per cent Amatol. They were all armed with a 1/10-of-a-second nose fuse and a 1/40-of-a-second specially prepared tail fuse. The 1/10-of-a-second nose fuse was provided in case the tail fuse failed. Eleven-second delay tail fuses were available to replace the 11/40-of-a-second tail fuse in case weather conditions made extremely low bombing necessary. In this case the tail fuse was to be changed just before take-off and the nose fuse in that case would not be armed.

The Chemical Warfare Service provided special incendiary clusters each containing 128 incendiary bombs. These clusters were developed at the Edgewood Arsenal and test dropped by the Air Corps test group at Aberdeen. Several tests were carried out to ensure their proper functioning and to determine the dropping angle and dispersion.

A special load of .50 calibre ammunition was employed. These consisted of one tracer, two armour piercing and three explosive rounds alternating through the load.[3]

The twenty-four aircraft prepared for the Tokyo raid were obtained from the 17th Bombardment Group. The fact that the bombers had been sourced from this group meant that it made sense to use its crews – they were, after all, experienced in the handling of the B-25.

This was explained to the Commanding Officer of the 17th Bombardment Group, Lieutenant Colonel W.C. Millis. He was told that this was to be a mission that would be extremely hazardous, would require a high degree of skill and would be of great value to America's war effort, but he was not informed of its purpose or target. It would be a mission no man could reasonably be ordered to carry out – volunteers only would be called for. Though they had no real idea what they were being asked to do, more men volunteered than could possibly be employed.

From these, twenty-four crews were selected and were ordered to report to Eglin Field in western Florida for a final period of training. These crews, together with the maintenance personnel, armourers, and so on, proceeded to Eglin Field as rapidly as the aircraft could be converted and made available. The first of them arrived just before 1 March, the rest soon after.

Once at Eglin Field, the men came under the command of Lieutenant Colonel Doolittle. Training then began in earnest for what would become the first joint action between the US Navy and the USAAF. More importantly, it would be the first strike back at the enemy.

Below: James H. Doolittle with the Curtiss R3C-2 Racer in which he won the 1925 Schneider Trophy Race. (NARA)

CHAPTER 2

Making it Happen

When the men were asked to volunteer for a secret mission, some of them guessed at the nature of the operation they would be undertaking. But it was not until all the crews had arrived at Eglin that a formal announcement was made by Colonel Doolittle that they were to fly from a carrier at sea to strike at Japan. The actual targets and target information would not be revealed, however, until they were aboard the carrier, the USS *Hornet*. It was also explained that, whilst only sixteen of the twenty-four B-25s would fly the mission, all twenty-four crews would be trained as if all were to participate in the raid. Likewise, all of the airmen would be embarked on *Hornet* to ensure complete security and just in case any of the designated crew members were taken ill or had to be replaced.

At the same time that the announcement of the mission was made, the training arrangements were also revealed, and concentrated courses of instruction duly began at Eglin Field. These included carrier take-off practice under the supervision of Lieutenant Henry Miller of the US Navy, this being undertaken on one of the auxiliary fields near Eglin. White lines were drawn on two of the runways of this field, representing the approximate length of the flight deck of a carrier.

Take-off practice was carried out with a light load, normal load, and overload up to 31,0000lbs. In all cases it was found that the shortest possible take-off was obtained with flaps full down, stabilizer set three-fourths, tail heavy, full power against the brakes and releasing the brakes simultaneously as the engine came up to revs. The control column was pulled back gradually, and the bomber left the ground with the tail skid about one foot from the runway. This appeared to be an unnatural attitude and the aircraft took off almost in a stall.

In spite of the high wing loading and unnatural attitude, the comparatively low power loading and good low-speed control characteristics of the B-25 made it possible to handle the aircraft without undue difficulty in such circumstances. The normal take-off speed for the Mitchell was between 105 and 110 miles per hour, but lift-off was achieved at lower speeds, with 69 miles per hour being the lowest recorded during training. Remarkably, only one pilot had difficulty during the take-off training. Taking off into a moderately gusty wind with full load, he permitted the B-25 to side slip back into the ground just after leaving the ground. No one was hurt, but the airplane was badly damaged.

As the pilots became more skilled, they were able to take-off at much shorter distances. The shortest measured take-off was accomplished by Lieutenant Don Smith who lifted off after just 287 feet.

Eventually, all the pilots achieved satisfactory take-offs at approximately 500 to 600 feet, loaded with 2,000lbs of bombs, a full gasoline load, full crew of five with combat equipment, and full armament. Though stripped of all unessential gear, each bomber was to carry its normal complement of five crew members, namely the pilot, a co-pilot, bombardier-navigator, radio operator and gunner-mechanic. One crew member was to be a competent meteorologist and another an experienced navigator. All navigators were to be trained in celestial navigation. Two ground liaison officers were also to be assigned. One would remain on the mainland and the other on the carrier. At least three crew members had to be able to speak Chinese, with one in each of the target units.

Special training was given in cross-country flying, night flying and navigation. Flights were made over the Gulf of Mexico in order to permit pilots and navigators to become accustomed to flying without visual or radio references and landmarks.

Low altitude approaches to bombing targets, rapid bombing and evasive action were performed. Bombing of land and sea targets was practised at heights of 1,500, 5,000 and 10,000 feet. As a rule, 100lb sand-filled bombs were used, though each crew was given an opportunity to bomb with live bombs as well.

The B-25B had only just been introduced into service and a number of teething problems were uncovered during the trials. For example, it had been found that when the turret guns were fired aft with the muzzle close to the fuselage the blast popped rivets and tore the skin loose. As a result of this it was necessary to install steel blast-plates.

Difficulty was also experienced in getting the lower turret to function properly. Trouble was encountered with the turret activating mechanism, as well as with the retracting and extending mechanism. These troubles were finally overcome to a large degree. However, it was then found that the attitude of the gunner and the operation of the sight were so difficult that it would not be possible in the time available to train gunners to efficiently operate the turret. As a consequence of this, and also in order to save weight and permit the installation of the additional fuel tanks, the lower turrets were removed, plates covering the hole where they had stuck through the bottom of the fuselage.

The experience of firing the remaining guns proved quite novel to the gunners who, almost without exception, had never fired a machine-gun from an aircraft at either a moving or stationary target, nor operated a power turret. Much practice was therefore required, but as there were no ground targets available, oil slicks were dropped on the surface of the sea at intervals of one and-a-half-miles which the gunners could aim at. The pilots were instructed to fly their aircraft in half turns from a firing position 100 to 200 feet from the water and at the same time circle one slick in a left bank then proceed to the next in a right bank which allowed the gunners to fire from one side to the other in order to become proficient in accuracy of firing as well as operating the turret.

Temporary targets were also set up on one of the auxiliary fields near Eglin. Sand bags and weights were placed in the tail of the B-25s to weight it to the ground in order for the top turret guns to be brought to bear on the ground targets.[4] In order to get practice in operating the turret, pursuit fighters – Curtiss P-36s and P-40s from Eglin Field – simulated attacks on the bombers and the gunners followed them with their empty guns. In each aircraft the engineers were trained as turret gunners and the bombardiers trained as nose gunners.

Despite a large amount of fog and bad weather which made flying impossible for days at a time, and the considerable amount of effort required to complete installations and make the aircraft operational at Eglin Field, the training proceeded rapidly under the direction of Captain Edward York. In fact, in just three weeks all of the men and machines were safely operational, although it

Overleaf: USS *Dunlap* passes close by the stern of USS *Enterprise* while operating at sea near the Hawaiian Islands on 8 April 1942, the same day that the carrier departed to take part in the Doolittle Raid on Japan. SBD scout-bombers of Bombing Squadron Six (VB-6) are being moved into position aft on the *Enterprise*'s flight deck. (USNHHC)

was noted that additional training of the crews and work on the aircraft might have improved their efficiency even further.

On 25 March 1942, the first of twenty-two aircraft took off from Eglin Field bound for Sacramento Air Depot. Two of the original twenty-four were missing. As previously mentioned, one of the B-25Bs was wrecked during take-off practice and another was damaged due to the failure of the front wheel shimmy damper. While taxying normally the front wheel shimmied so violently that a strut fitting failed and let the aircraft down on its nose. Although the damage was slight there was not time to repair it. Final fuel consumption tests and navigation training were incorporated into this flight to the Depot.

At Sacramento the bombers were given a final check over and their propellers were replaced with new ones. The crews were then given their last chance to fine-tune their flying techniques up and down the Sacramento valley. By 27 March, all of the aircraft had arrived and all special equipment, such as emergency rations, canteens, hatchets, knives, pistols and so on, were made secure.

As China was likely to be the place where the raiders would land, hopefully at Chuchow and then refuel to fly on to Chungking, it was calculated that the minimum distance of the flight would be 1,900 miles. For the bombers to be able to reach their targets and fly onto a safe landing in China,

Below: A map showing the general scheme for the Doolittle Raid. (NARA)

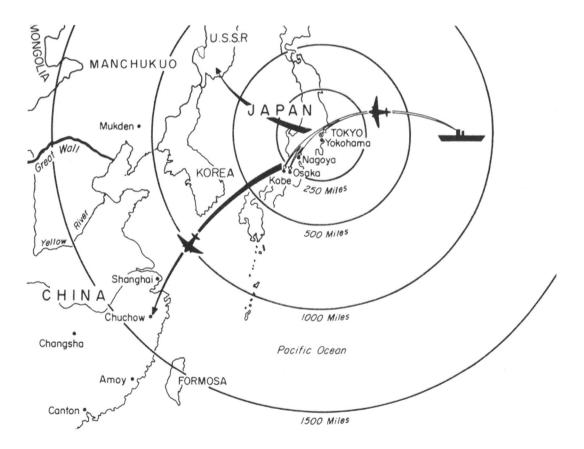

the greatest distance that *Hornet* could be from Tokyo would therefore be 400 miles. As the range of the modified B-25s was expected to be 2,200 miles, this allowed a comfortable margin for error. Fuel consumption, when fully loaded, was estimated to be seventy-eight gallons per hour, reducing to sixty-five gallons per hour as the load reduced.

For the aircraft to be flown on from their first landing to a safe place deeper in China, the aircraft would have to be refuelled. This would be an extremely dangerous time, as the Japanese would be certain to try to chase down the bombers and the Mitchells would be easy stationary targets.

To give the crews the best chance of resisting an attack, the old Wild West technique of circling the wagons was turned to. The aircraft would be refuelled in groups of three to form a circle and the engines kept running so that the upper gun turrets could still be operated. Mounts were also designed for the .30-calibre nose guns so that they could be removed from the nose and used for ground defence.

However, there was only time to fit a few of the bombers with these mounts because, on 31 March and 1 April 1942, some of the B-25s were to be loaded aboard the carrier USS *Hornet*. They were moving a step closer to taking part in one of the most audacious aerial missions of the Second World War.

Below: The various targets and landing grounds for the attack on 18 April 1942. (NARA)

CHAPTER 3

All at Sea

As the converted Mitchells were loaded on the USS *Hornet* at Naval Air Station Alameda on San Francisco Bay, the intention had always been, for reasons of space, to only stow fifteen of them. The reason why a sixteenth plane was taken was that Vice Admiral William F. 'Bull' Halsey, who was in charge of the task force which would accompany US *Hornet*, wanted each of the pilots to experience a carrier take-off at sea before the raid. As this was not possible, Halsey asked that the pilots at least got the chance to witness a carrier take-off. So, the extra, sixteenth, B-25 was taken

Above and opposite: The US Navy blimp *L-8* approaches USS *Hornet* to deliver parts for the mission's B-25Bs shortly after the carrier had left San Francisco, circa 4 April 1942. Note the package hanging below the airship. (USNHHC)

Above: With its delivery complete, *L-8* passes another of the ships in the task force as it heads back towards land. (NARA)

on board. This would take off during the first day out from port or on the first day of favourable weather afterwards and return to Alameda. This would give the pilot of the returning bomber an opportunity to relate his experiences by radio to the crews that would fly to Tokyo. However, it was soon agreed to retain this bomber on *Hornet* and increase the strike force by one.

The Naval force under Admiral Halsey was enumerated Task Force 16 and was split into two groups, Task Force 16.1 and Task Force 16.2. Halsey raised his flag in the aircraft carrier USS *Enterprise* (CV-6) which was the lead ship of TF 16.1. The other ships in this group were the cruisers USS *North Hampton* (CC-1) and USS *Salt Lake City* (CA-25), as well as the destroyers *Balch* (DD-363), *Benham* (DD-397), *Fanning* (DD-385) and *Ellet* (DD-398).

For its part, TF 16.2 was led by the all-important USS *Hornet*. The cruisers were USS *Vincennes* (CA-44) and USS *Nashville* (CL-43), which were supported by the destroyers *Gwin* (DD-433), *Grayson* (DD-435), *Meredith* (DD-434) and *Monssen* (DD-436).

Task Force 16.1 was accompanied by the tanker USS *Sabine* (AO-25). Task Force 16.2, meanwhile, was supported by the tanker USS *Cimaron* (AO-22).

The two groups were to sail independently and rendezvous at sea on 13 April. A strict policy of radio silence was to be maintained at all times throughout the task force.

USS *Hornet* had been launched on 14 December 1940, receiving her first aircraft in the Atlantic off Norfolk, Virginia, eleven days later at the start of her shake-down cruise into the Caribbean. When the B-25Bs were loaded onboard her by crane, most of the crew just assumed it was merely an exercise. It was not until 7 April, the sixth day at sea, that the naval operation plan, No.20-42 was issued, and the crew were informed of their mission.

Training with the raiding airmen, meanwhile, continued on the carrier as the task forces ploughed through the vast waters of the Pacific. This training consisted of a series of lectures on Japan, on first aid and sanitation, on gunnery, navigation and meteorology by members of the USAAF and a party of officers from *Hornet*, sprinkled with a series of inspirational talks by Doolittle himself.

There was also gunnery and turret practice in the aircraft sitting on the deck, using kites flown from *Hornet* for targets. Celestial navigation practice for the navigators was supervised by *Hornet*'s navigation officer. Star sights were taken from the deck and from the navigating compartment in the aircraft. In this way a high degree of proficiency was developed, and satisfactory optical characteristics of the navigating compartment window were assured.

A great deal of thought was given to the best method of attack. It was felt that a take-off about three hours before daylight, meaning that the bombers would arrive over Tokyo at the crack of dawn, would give the greatest security, provide ideal bombing conditions, assure the element of surprise and permit arrival at the final destination before dark. This plan was abandoned because of the anticipated difficulty of a night take-off from the carrier and also because the Navy was unwilling to light up the carrier deck for take-off in such dangerous waters.

Another suggestion was to take-off at the crack of dawn, bomb in the early morning and proceed to the destination, arriving before dark. This plan had the disadvantage of the bombing being made in daylight, presumably after the Japanese had already spotted the raiders arriving over their territory. There was a real risk in this plan of all the bombers being intercepted long before they were anywhere near Tokyo.

The third plan was to take-off just before dark, bomb at night and proceed to the destination, arriving there after daylight in the early morning. In order to make this plan practical, one B-25 was to take-off ahead of the others, arrive over Tokyo at dusk and target the most inflammable part of the city with incendiary bombs. This minimized the overall hazard and assured that the target would

Left: Some of the raiders' B-25Bs parked on the flight deck of USS *Hornet* while en route to the launching point. The Mitchell that can be seen upper right is that of crew No.8, which was commanded by Captain Edward York. Its serial number, #40-2242, is clearly visible on the tail. Note the use of the flight deck tie-down strips to secure the aircraft. The aircraft in this picture are positioned near the forward edge of the midships aircraft elevator. It is likely that the aircraft nearest the camera is that of Lieutenant Harold Watson's crew No.9. (USNHHC)

Above: Another view of the bombers tied down on the flight deck of USS *Hornet* while the carrier was at sea. The plane in the second row from the camera is that of Captain David Jones' crew No.5, serial number #40-2283. As there was no room to rearrange the B-25s, and their long, non-folding wings made it impossible to send them below, they were parked on *Hornet*'s flight deck in the order they were to depart on the day of the mission. (USNHHC)

Above: USS *Hornet*, as seen from USS *Salt Lake City*, running into rough weather while steaming at high speed en route to the launch point. (National Museum of the US Navy)

be lit up for the following aircraft. It was this strategy that was finally settled on, though it was also agreed with the Navy that if the task force was spotted by the Japanese, the bombers would take-off immediately, even if the desired launch time and distance to Tokyo had not been reached.

The Japanese, monitoring US Navy radio traffic, deduced that a carrier raid on the homeland was a possibility after 14 April 1942, and prepared accordingly. Consequently, as the task force steamed ever closer to the enemy's mainland the danger of encountering one of its ships was very real.

Indeed, as the darkened US ships sliced through heavy seas during the mid-watch on 18 April, USS *Enterprise* detected intruders on her radar, and at 03.15 hours signalled the other vessels ominously: 'Two enemy surface craft spotted'. The men of the task force manned their battle stations and lookouts and watch-keepers anxiously monitored the situation. Fortunately, these two vessels were avoided without them becoming aware of the US ships.

As the day dawned, cold and grey, at 07.38 hours lookouts spotted the Japanese picket boat 70-ton *No.23 Nitto Maru* at a distance of 20,000 yards in a position about 668 miles from Tokyo.

Above: USS *Nashville* also photographed from USS *Salt Lake City* whilst TF 16.2, of which *Hornet* was a part, was steaming towards Japan. (National Museum of the US Navy)

Although this patrol boat was sunk, it was believed that its crew had managed to send at least one sighting report.

There was nothing for it – the bombers would have to take-off without delay, even though *Hornet* was still some 650 nautical miles from Japan, and approximately 824 miles east of the centre of Tokyo. This was almost double the distance it had been expected that the raiders would have to fly to reach the Japanese capital. This meant that the 300-mile safety allowance would be swallowed up and that there was no longer any chance of the B-25s reaching the proposed landing grounds in China.

There was no hesitation amongst any of the crews. They knew that they would most likely have to ditch. If they were lucky, they might reach the Chinese mainland, but would almost be certain to fall into the hands of the enemy. It really was a case of the devil or the deep blue sea.

The bulk of the task force immediately set course away from Japan. In the afternoon it was obliged to sink two more Japanese surface craft that were encountered. It is of interest to note that even at this distance from Japan the ocean was apparently studded with enemy vessels.

Right: Lieutenant Colonel James H. Doolittle (standing left front) and Captain Marc A. Mitscher, Commanding Officer of USS *Hornet*, pose with a 500lb bomb and USAAF aircrew members during ceremonies on *Hornet*'s flight deck while the raid task force was en route to the launching point. (USNHHC)

Below: On 16 April, whilst *Hornet* was en route to the launching point, a ceremony was held on the carrier's deck during which, notes one official account, 'several medals were tied to a single 500lb bomb that would be dropped by Ted Lawson's *Ruptured Duck*. The ceremony served to ease the tensions, but only for a brief time.' (USNHHC)

Above: Part of the cargo of bombs loaded on USS *Hornet* waiting to be transferred to the carrier's flight deck to be loaded onto the B-25s. (NARA)

Above: One of the bombs for Doolittle's B-25s on the flight deck prior to the armourers loading it on to one of the bombers. (NARA)

Above: A close up of one of the medals attached to the 500lb bomb by Doolittle. The medals themselves had been donated by Lieutenant Stephen Jurika, who had, as a US Navy officer, received them during his pre-war naval attaché service and 'now wished to pointedly return them to a hostile government'. (National Museum of the US Navy)

Below: As well as one of the medals supplied by Lieutenant Stephen Jurika, this 500lb bomb has also been annotated with notes and comments written by the crew of USS *Hornet*. (NARA)

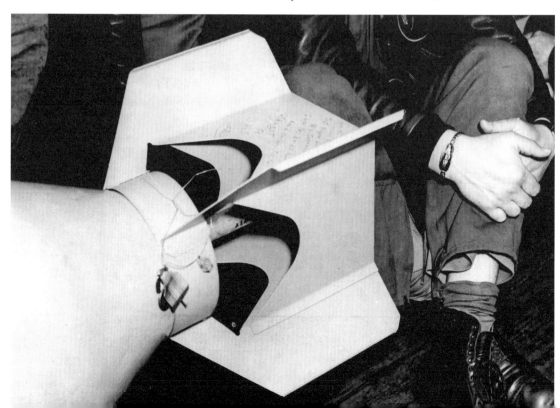

Above: Presumably another photograph taken on 16 April whilst *Hornet* was at sea, in this shot Doolittle (left front) can be seen in discussion with Captain Marc A. Mitscher. (USNHHC)

Below: A picture taken looking aft down *Hornet's* flight deck, as seen from the rear of the island. The B-25 in the foreground is #40-2203, which was flown by crew No.9 (Lieutenant Watson). Just visible on the far right is the tail of #40-2250, this being the mount of crew No.10 (Lieutenant Joyce). Both of these crews attacked targets in the Tokyo area. (USNHHC)

Main image: A number of the B-25s parked on the flight deck of USS *Hornet*. (USNHHC)

29

Above: Aircrewmen preparing .50-calibre machine-gun ammunition on the flight deck of USS *Hornet* while the carrier was steaming toward the mission's launching point. Three of the B-25B bombers are visible. That in the upper left is #40-2298, which was piloted by Lieutenant Dean E. Hallmark of crew No.6. In the background is # 40-2283 of Jones' crew No.5. (USNHHC)

Opposite: A close-up of some of the men preparing the ammunition for the B-25s. The ammunition box to the right is marked 'A.P. M2, Incndy. M1, Trcr. M1'. This indicates that the ammunition types inside are armour piercing, incendiary and tracer. Note the wooden flight deck planking, with metal aircraft tie-down strips in place of every eighth plank. (USNHHC)

Main Image: A photograph taken looking aft from the island of USS *Hornet* while the task force was en route to the raiders' launching point. USS *Gwin* is coming alongside, as USS *Nashville* steams in the distance. Eight of the mission's sixteen B-25B bombers are parked within view, as are two of the ship's Douglas SBD scout bombers. Note the midships elevator, torpedo elevator, arresting gear and flight deck barriers in the lower portion of the photograph, as well as the quad anti-aircraft machine-gun mount to the left. (USNHHC)

Above: USS *Fanning* escorting the aircraft carrier USS *Enterprise* on the day the Doolittle Raid aircraft were launched, 18 April 1942. Halsey had raised his flag on *Enterprise* which was the lead ship of TF 16.1. The photograph was taken from USS *Salt Lake City*. The destroyer in the background, steaming towards the left, is USS *Balch*. (USNHHC)

Below: USS *Gwin*, part of the escorts for TF 16.2, approaches USS *Hornet* from astern, with the cruiser USS *Nashville* beyond. The ships are framed by the tail of one of the B-25s parked on the rear of the carrier's flight deck. (USNHHC)

Above: Another picture taken looking aft and to port from the island of USS *Hornet*. The cruiser USS *Vincennes* is in the distance. The B-25 in the foreground is #40-2261, which was flown by crew No.7 (Lieutenant Lawson), whilst the next aircraft is crew No.8's #40-2242. (USNHHC)

Main Image: Again pictured from USS *Salt Lake City* on 18 April 1942, the destroyer USS *Fanning* is seen manoeuvring near USS *Enterprise*. (USNHHC)

Above: Two of the operation's bombers pictured whilst parked on the flight deck of USS *Hornet*. The B-25 on the right, #40-2282, was flown by Lieutenant Everett W. Holstrom and his crew No.4. Note protective cover over its gun turret, and the wooden dummy machine-guns mounted in its tail cone. The second Mitchell on the left is warming up its engines, as was done periodically during the voyage. (USNHHC)

Above: The nose of one of the raiders' B-25s pictured whilst it is tied down on the flight deck of USS *Hornet* while en route to the take-off point. This aircraft, #40-2249, is that of Captain Greening's crew No.11. Nicknamed *Hari Carrier*, it has been given appropriate nose art. Note the slippage mark on the nosewheel and tyre, and inscription on the wheel cover which states 'Inflating instructions inside; check tire pressure daily'. (USNHHC)

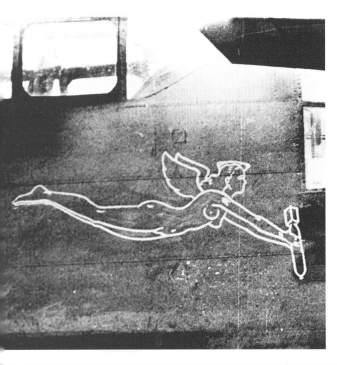

Left: Another view of the nose art applied to Captain Greening's B-25, #40-2249 nicknamed *Hari Carrier*. (USNHHC)

Below: Some B-25s and *Hornet*'s Grumman F4F-3 Wildcat fighters on the flight deck while the task force was en route to the launching point. Note the wooden dummy machine-guns in the tail cone of the B-25. (USNHHC)

Opposite page top: Eight of the Doolittle Raiders' sixteen B-25s are visible on flight deck of USS *Hornet*. The aircraft to the right is Lieutenant Joyce's #40-2250. During the two-week-long outward passage, the bombers received regular maintenance and engine testing to ensure they would be ready. (USNHHC)

Opposite page bottom: The B-25s packed in at the rear of *Hornet*'s flight deck. (National Museum of the US Navy)

Above: USS *Sabine* refuels USS *Enterprise* in rough weather during the approach phase of the mission, 17 April 1942. Note the configuration of refuelling gear, and the spare anchor stowed on the oiler's after superstructure bulkhead. (USNHHC)

Opposite page top: The two carriers, USS *Hornet* (foreground) and USS *Enterprise*, pictured together, from the deck of USS *Salt Lake City*, prior to the departure of the B-25s. (National Museum of the US Navy)

Opposite page bottom: Crewmen work on a B-25 parked at the very rear of USS *Hornet*'s flight deck. It is possible that this aircraft, #40-2268, was that flown by Lieutenant Farrow and the men of crew No.16. One of the escorts, USS *Gwin*, can be seen approaching the carrier from astern. (USNHHC)

Above: One of the B-25s tied down on the deck of USS *Hornet*. This is almost certainly #40-2344, which was flown by Lieutenant Colonel Doolittle and his crew. (NARA)

Below: Surrounded by the tied-down Raiders' B-25s, the engine of Douglas SBD Dauntless parked on *Hornet*'s deck is warmed up as the task force steams towards the launch point. (NARA)

PART TWO

Target Japan

Saturday, 18 April 1942

Above: One of the B-25s lines up for take-off from USS *Hornet* on the morning of 18 April 1942. Note the white lines painted on the flight deck, below the bomber's nose and port side wheels, to guide the pilot during his take-off run. This is the 3rd, Lieutenant Gray's aircraft, or 4th B-25, Lieutenant Holtrom's, to be launched. (USNHHC)

As the B-25s' moment of departure neared, final instructions were given to the crews to avoid non-military targets and, even though the aircraft were unlikely to reach the Chinese coast they were told that they would be ill-advised to land anywhere in the Soviet Union. They were to fly as far west as possible, land on the water, launch their dinghies and try to sail on. All special equipment such as emergency rations, canteens, hatchets, knives, pistols, etc. were made secure before take-off.

The skipper of each aircraft was also given $500 to use, if necessary, to bribe the Chinese to help them reach Chuchow. 'The planes were prepared, the cruisers were prepared, the bombs were loaded, the fuels were topped off,' wrote Tom Casey of the Doolittle Tokyo Raiders Association. 'Everything was done and in a little over an hour Doolittle was sitting in position, the *Hornet* was turned into the wind, 30-foot seas, there was a pretty good breeze blowing across the deck.'[5]

Upon take-off each aircraft climbed to the right height and flew over *Hornet* lining the

Right: The Doolittle Raid underway as at least five or six B-25s remain on the flight deck of USS *Hornet* waiting for their turn to take-off on the morning of 18 April 1942. (USNHHC)

Below: Having just taken-off from the carrier, one of the B-25s flies over USS *Hornet* whilst setting course for Japan on the morning of 18 April 1942. (USNHHC)

Above: As one of USS *Enterprise*'s battle group, the cruiser USS *Northampton* eventually joined the task force assigned to the Doolittle Raid. She is pictured here refuelling from USS *Cimarron* on 18 April 1942. (USNHHC)

axis of the ship up with the drift sight. The course of the carrier was displayed in large figures from the gun turret abaft the island. This meant that, in the featureless ocean, the navigators were able to get an accurate fix before setting off across the hundreds of miles across the Pacific.

All of the pilots were given selected objectives, variously consisting of steel works, oil refineries, oil tank farms, ammunition dumps, dock yards, munitions plants, airplane factories, etc. They were also given secondary targets in case it was impossible to reach the primary objectives.

In addition to each B-25 crew having selected targets assigned to it, each flight of three bombers was allocated a specific course and general area to cover. The first flight, led by Lieutenant Hoover, was given the northern part of Tokyo, with the second flight, commanded by Captain Jones, being allocated the central part of Tokyo. The third flight, led by Captain York, had the southern part of Tokyo and the north central part of the Tokyo bay area, whilst the fourth flight, led by Captain Greening, was to cover the southern part of Kanagawa, the city of Yokohama and the Yokosuka Navy Yard. The final, fifth, flight was directed to head around to the South of Tokyo and proceed to the vicinity of Nagoya.

The flights were spread over a fifty-mile-wide front in order to provide the greatest possible coverage, to create the impression that there was a larger number of bombers than were actually airborne, and to dilute enemy ground and air fire. This plan also prohibited the possibility of more than one B-25 passing any given spot on the ground and assured the element of surprise.

The best information available from Army and Navy intelligence sources indicated that there were some 500 combat aircraft in Japan. Most of these were, it was believed, concentrated in the Tokyo

Bay area. It was also anticipated that some difficulty might be experienced due to the targets being camouflaged, though, in reality, little or no effective camouflage was observed in the Tokyo area.

As the bombers flew on, there were other encounters with the Japanese. The first of these occurred when the bombers passed a Japanese light cruiser to the east of Tokyo, after which they encountered a Japanese patrol aircraft which was headed directly for the task force about 600 miles from Tokyo. This 'plane turned around and followed one of the Mitchells, so it is certain that the raiders were observed by it. Despite these incidents, and the fact that the raiders flew over innumerable patrol and fishing boats from some 300 miles off-shore until crossing the enemy coast, the Japanese were apparently entirely unprepared for the raiders' arrival.

From this moment onwards, the success and survival of each of the Doolittle raiders was in the hands of the individual crews. As a result, let us now follow each one of the B-25s in turn as they made their attack on the Japanese archipelago.

Below: Holding his launch flag, one of *Hornet*'s Flight Deck Officers, visible on the right, provides instructions to the crew of one of the raiders during its last few seconds on the deck of the carrier. For each crew, the launching officer timed the start of the take-off roll to ensure that it reached the forward end of the flight deck as the ship pitched up in the heavy seas, thus giving extra lift at a critical instant. Once again, note the white stripes painted on the flight deck to guide the pilot's alignment of his aircraft's nose and port side wheels. (USNHHC)

Previous spread: The first of four photographs that may well show the same B-25 taking-off from USS *Hornet*. (NARA)

Left: The B-25 pictured the moment that it lifts off from the flight deck. (NARA)

Above: The bomber climbs up, the engines no doubt at full power. (NARA)

Below: Next stop Japan! (NARA)

Above: One of the Doolittle Raiders pictured at the moment it has taken-off from USS *Hornet* on the morning of 18 April 1942. The leading B-25, that piloted by Doolittle himself, had but a few hundred feet of deck run to reach flying speed, but every subsequent one had a little more. (USNHHC)

Below: Seen from the far end of the flight deck, one of the first raiders takes-off from *Hornet*. The rest of the attackers waiting for their turn can be seen behind. (NARA)

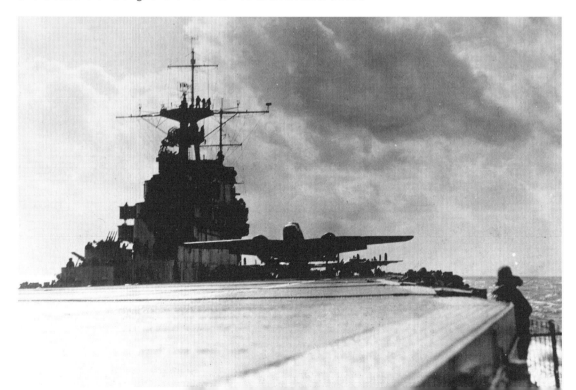

Above: Some of the B-25s pictured heading from Japan having formed-up after taking-off from USS *Hornet* on 18 April 1942. The smaller specks in the sky are US Navy patrol aircraft which took part in the first phase of the operation. (US National Museum of the US Navy)

Below: One of the last of the B-25s to get airborne passes over the end of the flight deck as it takes off, bound for Japan. (NARA)

Above and below: The same B-25 snapped a second or two after the previous image taken on USS *Salt Lake City*. (National Museum of the US Navy)

Opposite page top: Some of USS *Hornet*'s crew watch from a signal lamp platform as one of the B-25s gets airborne at the start of its journey to the heart of Japan. (USNHHC)

Opposite page bottom: One of the Doolittle Raiders passes over USS *Salt Lake City* on 18 April 1942, whilst, in the words of the original caption, 'heading for Japan for the first taste of war on their own islands'. (National Museum of the US Navy)

Above: Taken on 4 April 1942, a few days before the Raid, this photograph shows the forward flight deck of USS *Enterprise* with Douglas SBD Dauntless and Grumman F4F Wildcat aircraft. During their deployment on 18 April, these aircraft damaged the armed merchant cruiser *Awata Maru* and the picket-boats *Chokyu Maru, No.1 Iwate Maru, No.2 Asami Maru, Kaijin Maru, No.3 Chinyo Maru, Eikichi Maru, Kowa Maru,* and *No.21 Nanshin Maru.* (USNHHC)

Opposite page: Also on 18 April, in a series of actions often over-shadowed by the other events that day, aircraft from USS *Enterprise* attacked Japanese picket boats located near TF-16. The carrier had launched the Grumman F4F-3A Wildcats of VF-6, to undertake combat air patrols, as well as the Douglas SBD-3s of VB-3 and SBD-2s of VB-6. This view shows Wildcats and Douglas TBD Devastators packing the flight deck of USS *Enterprise* as she steams towards Japanese waters, on 11 April 1942, to take part in the Doolittle Raid. (USNHHC)

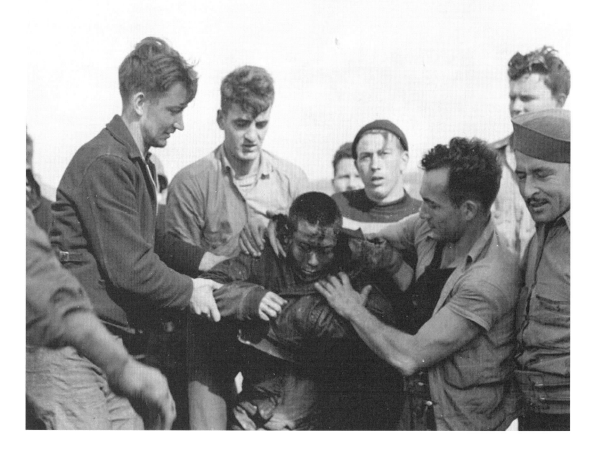

Opposite page top: As well as being attacked by the 'planes from *Enterprise*, two other picket-boats, *No.23 Nitto Maru* (which had transmitted the initial contact report) and *Nagato Maru*, were sunk by gunfire of the light cruiser USS *Nashville*. This image shows *Nashville*, part of TF 16.2, firing her main guns at one of the picket boats encountered by the task force on 18 April 1942. (USNHHC)

Opposite page bottom: Crewman from USS *Nashville* support a Japanese seaman rescued from the water after the sinking of one of the enemy picket boats. (NARA)

Below: An SBD-3 Dauntless of VB-6 preparing for take-off on USS *Enterprise* early in 1942. During the various engagements with USS *Enterprise*'s aircraft on 18 April, the Japanese downed one of the carrier's SBD-3s. This was the Dauntless flown by Ensign Liston R. Comer, USNR, of VB-6. Having ditched, the crew was rescued by a destroyer. The next day, 19 April, the picket boat *No.21 Nanshin Maru*, badly damaged by the US aircraft, was scuttled by gunfire of the light cruiser *Kiso*. At the same time, *No.1 Iwate Maru* sank as the result of damage inflicted the day before. The Doolittle Raid had temporarily put that section of the Japanese navy's offshore warning network out of commission. (USNHHC)

Above: Pilots of Bombing Squadron Three pictured onboard USS *Enterprise* during April 1942. Standing in the back row, third from left, is Ensign John C. Butler USNR. On 18 April, Butler flew one of *Enterprise*'s SBD-3 Dauntless, S-12, with ARM3c David D. Berg as his radio-gunner. Their role, once airborne, was to patrol and search for any forward deployed Japanese ships that could radio warning of the inbound raiders. During this scouting mission, Ensign Butler engaged a 125-foot long Japanese patrol boat towing a smaller boat 'painted white'. Attacking in two separate dives, Butler dropped two 100lb bombs, both of 'which were duds'. Striking the craft with a 500lb bomb on the port side, Butler's Dauntless received three hits from enemy fire. Disengaging, Butler noticed the smaller craft belching oil and smoke, and stated that he believed it later sank. The larger boat remained undamaged.

Butler was subsequently killed in action during the Battle of Midway in June 1942, during an action for which he was posthumously awarded the Navy Cross. Such were their exploits during the Pacific War, that six of the men in this picture later had ships named after them, Ensign Butler being one. (USNHHC)

KEY TO THE FOLLOWING CREW PHOTOGRAPHS – PAGES 65 - 113

+   Killed baling out over China, 18 April 1942
*   Killed in crash, 18 April 1942
•   Prisoner of War of the Japanese for 3½ years
++   Executed by the Japanese, 15 October 1942
**   Died in Japanese prison, 1 December 1943
••   Survived the mission, returned, but killed/died later in the war
••• Survived the mission, but killed/died in service after the war

---

Crew No.1
B-25 Mitchell #40-2344
Crew brought together as part of 34th Bombardment Squadron
Target Tokyo

Left to right: Lieutenant Henry A. Potter (navigator)
Lieutenant Colonel James H. Doolittle (pilot and mission commander)
Staff Sergeant Fred A. Braemer (bombardier)
Lieutenant Richard E. Cole (co-pilot)
Staff Sergeant Paul J. Leonard (flight engineer/gunner) ••

Above: Doolittle rests on the ground by the wing of his B-25, #40-2344, on a Chinese hillside. (NARA)

oolittle's B-25B was the first of the raiders to take-off at 08.20 hours. As *Hornet* swung about and prepared to launch the bombers, which had been readied for take-off the previous day, a gale of more than 40 knots churned the sea with thirty-foot crests. Heavy swells, which caused the ship to pitch violently, shipped sea and spray over the bow, and drenched the deck crews.

Despite the conditions, Doolittle powered his heavily-laden bomber down the flight deck. Many of the men tensely watching momentarily feared the worst when the bomber suddenly dropped in altitude, only to then rise back up. Having circled *Hornet*, Doolittle set a course for Japan.

Doolittle's official summary of what followed was somewhat brief. It read as follows: 'Proceeded to Tokyo and bombed the North Central industrial area with 4 incendiary clusters. Proceeded on to the China Coast where very unfavourable weather made it necessary for crew to abandon ship. Put plane on A.F.C.E. [Automatic Flight Control Equipment] and turned off gasoline valves. Pilot jumped last at 00.20 hours ship time, from 8,000 feet and landed near Tien Mu Shen, about 70 miles north of Chuchow. After landing contacted General Ho, Director of the Western Branch of Chekiang Province who agreed to take the necessary steps to collect missing crew members, locate the ship and establish a look-out for other planes in China, on the stretch of beach between Hung Chow Bay and Wen Chow Bay and by the sampans and junks that might be putting out to sea. All crew members o.k.'

In due course, Doolittle also penned a more descriptive personal report. It is also worth including here: 'Take-off was easy. Night take-off would have been possible and practicable. Circled carrier to get exact heading and check compass. Wind was from around 300 degrees.

'About a half hour after take-off was joined by AC 40-2292, Lieutenant Hoover, pilot, the second plane to take-off. About an hour out, passed a Japanese camouflaged naval surface vessel of about 6,000 tons. Took it to be a light cruiser.

'About two hours out passed a multi-motored land plane headed directly for our flotilla and flying at about 3,000 ft., 2 miles away. Passed and endeavoured to avoid various civil and naval craft until land fall was made north of Inubo Shuma. Was somewhat north of desired course but decided to take advantage of error and approach from a northerly direction, thus avoiding anticipated strong opposition to the west.

'Many flying fields and the air full of planes north of Tokyo. Mostly small biplanes, apparently primary or basic trainers. Encountered nine fighters in three flights of three. This was about ten miles north of the outskirts of Tokyo proper. All this time had been flying as low as the terrain would permit.

'Continued low flying due south over the outskirts of and toward the east centre of Tokyo. Pulled up to 1,200 ft., changed course to the southwest and incendiary-bombed highly inflammable section. Dropped first bomb at 13:30 (ship time).'

Doolittle's crew had made history, with the first American offensive strike against the Japanese mainland underway. The enemy defences, however, were not found wanting, as Doolittle went to note:

'Anti-aircraft [fire] very active but only one near hit. Lowered away to housetops and slid over western outskirts into low haze and smoke. Turned south and out to sea. Fewer airports on west side but many army posts.

'Passed over small aircraft factory with a dozen or more newly completed planes on the line. No bombs left. Decided not to machine gun for reasons of personal security.

'Had seen five barrage balloons over east central Tokyo and what appeared to be more in the distance. Passed on out to sea flying low.

'Was soon joined again by Hoover who followed us to the Chinese coast. Navigator plotted perfect course to pass north of Yaki Shima. Saw three large naval vessels just before passing west end of Japan. One was flatter than the others and may have been a converted carrier. Passed innumerable fishing and small patrol boats.

'Made land fall somewhat north of course on China coast. Tried to reach Chuchow but couldn't raise. It had been clear over Tokyo but became overcast before reaching Yaki Shima.

'Ceiling lowered on coast until low islands and hills were in it at about 600 feet. Just getting dark and couldn't live under overcast so pulled up to 6,000 and then 8,000 feet in it. On instruments from then on though occasionally saw dim lights on ground through almost solid overcast. These lights seemed more often on our right and pulled us still farther off course.

'Directed rear gunner to go aft and secure films from camera (unfortunately they were jerked out of his shirt front where he had put them, when his chute opened).

'Decided to abandon ship. Sergeant Braemer, Lieutenant Potter, Sergeant Leonard and Lieutenant Cole jumped in order. Left ship on A.F.C.E., shut off both gas cocks and I left. Should have put flaps down. This would have slowed down landing speed, reduced impact and shortened glide.

'All hands collected, and our plane located by late afternoon of 19th.

'Requested General Ho Yang Ling, Director of the Branch Government of Western Chekiang Province to have a lookout kept along the seacoast from Hang Chow bay to Wen Chow bay and also have all sampans and junks along the coast keep a lookout for planes that went down at sea, or just reached shore.

'Early morning of 20th four planes and crews, in addition to ours, had been located and I wired General Arnold, through the Embassy at Chungking, "Tokyo successfully bombed. Due to bad weather on China Coast believe all airplanes wrecked. Five crews found safe in China so far." Wired again on the 27th giving more details.

'Discussed possibility of purchasing three prisoners on the seacoast from Puppet Government and endeavouring to take out the three in the lake area by force. Believe this desire was made clear to General Ku Cho-tung (who spoke little English) and I know it was made clear to English-speaking members of his staff. This was at Shangjao. They agreed to try purchase of three, but recommended against force due to large Japanese concentration.

'Left aircraft about 21.20 hours (ship time) after 13 hours in the air. Still had enough gas for half hour flight but right front tank was showing empty. Had transferred once as right engine used more fuel. Had covered about 2,250 miles, mostly at low speed, cruising but about an hour at moderate high speed which more than doubled the consumption for this time.'

Having written the above, Doolittle then reflected in the positive and negative lessons of the raid. Of the latter, which he referred to as 'bad luck', he singled out three points: '(1) Early take-off due to naval contact with surface and aircraft; (2) Clear over Tokyo. (3) Foul over China.' In terms of 'good luck', he remarked on '(1) A 25mph tailwind over most of the last 1,200 miles'.

In concluding his account, Doolittle made the following observations: 'Take-off should have been made three hours before daylight, but we didn't know how easy it would be and the Navy didn't want to light up. Dawn take-off, closer in, would have been better as things turned out. However, due to the bad weather it is questionable if even daylight landing could have been made at Chuchow without radio aid. Still feel that original plan of having one plane take off three hours before dusk and others just at dusk was best all-around plan for average conditions.

'Should have kept accurate chronological record. Should have all crew members instructed in *exact* method of leaving ship under various conditions.'

In a memo to 'Hap' Arnold on 5 June 1942, Doolittle provided the following additional information: 'The comparatively few fighters actually encountered indicated that home defence had been reduced in the interest of making the maximum number of planes available in active theatres elsewhere. The pilots of such planes as remained appeared inexperienced. In some cases, they actually did not attack, and in many cases failed to drive the attack home to the maximum extent possible. In no case was there any indication that a Japanese pilot might run into one of our planes even though the economics of such a course would appear sound. It would entail trading a $40,000 fighter for a $200,000 bomber and one man, who could probably arrange to collide in such a way as to save himself, against five who even though they escaped would be interned and thus lose their military utility.

'The fire of the pilots that actually attacked was very inaccurate. In some cases, the machine-gun bullets bounced off the wings without penetrating them. This same effect was observed when a train, upon which some of our crew members were riding in China, was machine gunned by a Japanese attack plane. One of the projectiles which had bounced off the top of the train without penetrating was recovered. It was a steel pellet about one inch long, pointed on one end and boat-tailed on the other. It had no rifling marks and was apparently fired from a smooth bore gun.

'The anti-aircraft defense was active but inaccurate. All anti-aircraft bursts were black and apparently small guns of about 37mm or 40mm size. It is presumed that the high speed and low altitude at which we were flying made it impossible for them to train their larger calibre guns on us

Above: Chinese soldiers examine the wreckage of Doolittle's B-25 in the immediate aftermath of the attack on 18 April 1942. The aircraft crashed in Haotianguan, where Zhejiang Province meets Anhui Province. Five of the crew baled out and came down in the Tianmushan area of Lin'an County, Zhejiang Province. (NARA)

Below: A severed wing from B-25 #40-2344, the aircraft used by Doolittle and his crew No.1, lies in the Chinese countryside. Having baled out, Doolittle sought shelter overnight in a paddy field where he was discovered the following day by a group of students. He was escorted to the Western Zhejiang Administration, where he re-joined the rest of crew. (NARA)

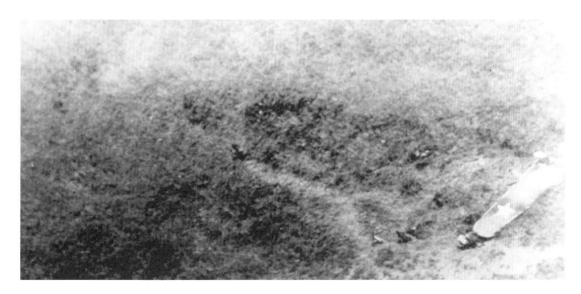

if such existed. Several of the airplanes were struck by anti-aircraft fragments but none of them was damaged to an extent that impaired their utility or impeded their progress.

'Although it was to be presumed that machine gun fire from the ground was active, none of the crew members interviewed to date saw any such action nor was there evidence of machine gun fires in the bottom of any of the airplanes. A few barrage balloons were seen. One cluster of five or six was observed just north of the Northernmost part of Tokyo Bay and what appeared to be another cluster was observed near the Bay to the Southeast. These barrage balloons were flying at about 3000 feet and were not in sufficient numbers to impede our bombing. Japanese anti-aircraft fire was so inaccurate that when shooting at one of our airplanes in the vicinity of the barrage balloons they actually shot down some of their own balloons.'[6]

Above: Lieutenant Colonel James H. Doolittle with members of his crew and Chinese officials in China after the attack. Those present are, from left to right: Staff Sergeant Fred A. Braemer; Staff Sergeant Paul J. Leonard; General Ho, director of the Branch Government of Western Chekiang Province; Lieutenant Richard E. Cole; Lieutenant Colonel Doolittle; Henry H. Shen, bank manager; Lieutenant Henry A. Potter; and Chao Foo Ki, secretary of the Western Chekiang Province Branch Government. (USNHHC)

Crew No.2
B-25 Mitchell #40-2292
Crew brought together as part of 37th Bombardment Squadron
Target Tokyo

Left to right: Lieutenant Carl R. Wildner (navigator)
Lieutenant Travis Hoover (pilot)
Lieutenant Richard E. Miller (bombardier)••
Lieutenant William N. Fitzhugh (co-pilot)
Sergeant Douglas V. Radney (flight engineer/gunner)

The second raider to lift off from USS *Hornet*, at 08.25 hours, was 40-2292 flown by Lieutenant Travis Hoover. Doolittle wrote that this was the only aircraft which experienced any difficulty in taking-off:

'The sea was so rough that water was being taken on over the bow of the carrier, and the take-off was made on the upbeat. The airplane was thrown into the air and the pilot pulled back on the stick too abruptly. For a moment it looked as though the plane might fall off on a wing but through good piloting Lieutenant Hoover was able to correct the condition and proceed without further difficulty. This together with the Navy crew member who was struck in the arm by a propeller while assisting in manoeuvring an airplane on the deck, was the only eventuality during take-off. Both were due to the rough sea. (After this take-off Lieutenant Miller recommended a more normal take off to the other pilots.)

'Proceeded to Tokyo and bombed powder factories and magazines near the river north of the main railroad station and Imperial Palace with 3 demolition bombs and one incendiary cluster. This bombing was done from 900 feet, and the debris flew to a height higher than that of the airplane. Proceeded to a point on the China coast near Ninypo.'

Hoover had caught up with Doolittle soon after take-off and accompanied 40-2234 all the way to Japan, making landfall around thirty miles north of Tokyo. The two bombers flew down the coast together, passing over the Imperial Palace before reaching the target area at 12.15 hours. Miller released the B-25's payload without opposition and then turned south-west to China.

Hoover reached Chinese territory but with one engine not working and almost out of fuel, he knew he would not be able to clear the mountains he saw looming ahead. The problem was that the aircraft was too low for the men to bale out, leaving Hoover with only one option – a forced landing. No solid and even ground could be found, so Hoover had to put the Mitchell down in a paddy field.

Remarkably, Hoover landed his aircraft relatively smoothly, the bomber coming to a gentle halt as it slid to a standstill in the muddy field. The crew collected all the equipment they might need to help them find their way to Chuchow and then set fire to the 'plane. They had landed near the port city of Ningbo, Zhejiang Province, which was then an area occupied by the Japanese army, but they were discovered by Chinese guerrillas and escorted to safety.

Left: Tung-Sheng 'Tom' Liu, standing third from the right in the white jacket, stands with the crew of Lieutenant Travis Hoover. Liu helped these men escape capture following the Raid, guiding them through Japanese-occupied territory to a dusty landing strip from where they were flown to safety. 'During our whole trip under Liu's guidance, our treatment was superb,' recalled Lieutenant Wildner. 'He had risked his neck for us.' After the war, Liu immigrated to the United States and was one of four individuals subsequently named as honorary Doolittle Raiders. He passed away in Los Angeles in May 2009. (US Air Force)

Crew No.3
B-25 Mitchell #40-2270
Crew brought together as part of 95th Bombardment Squadron
Target Tokyo

Left to right: Lieutenant Charles J. Ozuk Jr. (navigator)
Lieutenant Robert M. Gray (pilot)••
Sergeant Aden E. Jones (bombardier)
Lieutenant Jacob E. Manch (co-pilot)•••
Corporal Leland D. Faktor (flight engineer/gunner)+

Lieutenant Robert Gray's aircraft, named *Whisky Pete*, was the third away, at 08.30 hours. Once again, Doolittle's official report reveals the part he and his crew played in the attack:

'Proceeded to Tokyo. Bombed steel works, Gas Company and chemical works with demolition bombs and a factory district with incendiary bombs.

'Proceeded to China bailing [*sic*] out at 6,200 feet in the mountains near and Southeast of Chuchow. Lieutenant Gray, Lieutenant Manch and Sergeant Jones were uninjured. Lieutenant Ozuk suffered a severe cut on his leg due to landing on a sharp rock. Corporal L.D. Faktor was found dead. The case of Corporal Faktor's death was unknown as his parachute apparently functioned properly. It is suspected that he landed on extremely rough terrain and was killed in the secondary fall.'

When he hit the ground, Lieutenant Ozuk's parachute caught on the side of a cliff and he was hung suspended in his harness for more than twenty-four hours before being rescued by the Chinese.

Lieutenant Gray also provided his own brief account of his service with Colonel Doolittle: 'This mission was voluntary, called from Lexington Field, Columbia, S.C. and then to Eglin Field, Florida, to start working and training. From Florida the group went to McClellan Field, Cal. for more supplies and maintenance. We continued to Alameda Naval Base and loaded the planes aboard the U.S.S. *Hornet*. All navigation equipment was issued en route.

'Orders were given for all army pilots to man their planes for take-off. We were to report to Chuchow, China, as soon as possible if could not land our planes.'

Gray was ordered to bomb at an altitude of 1,500 feet, though his actual approach was below that height – in fact he did so at just 50 feet, releasing his payload at 1,450 feet. He lifted to 6,500 feet when over China.

Conditions were good on the approach to the target with broken cloud, becoming clearer as he approached Tokyo. The weather changed as 40-2270 flew towards China, where it was overcast and rainy. Gray's targets were given as 'Steel mill, chemical factory, gas co, and thickly populated small factories district.'

His Mission Report continued: 'Bombed Steel works but did not see the bombs hit. Felt the concussion. Second bomb made direct on gas company.

'Third bomb was a direct hit on the chemical works and setting fire to the whole works. Fourth scattered incendiary over the correct area but did not stay to see if it started fires. Machine gunned barracks and men on the way out.'

Gray also described his arrival over China: 'Giving orders thirty (30) minutes before time to bail [*sic*] out all personnel were in chutes. Gave an order fifteen (15) minutes before time again to make sure. When all personnel was gone, I switched on AFCE and jumped (6200 ft). I landed on summit of a mountain and remained there the remainder of the night.

'The next morning I looked for other personnel but could not find them. Walked all day and came to village where I stayed that night. Was directed in wrong direction for six miles and ended up where I started from that morning. Sergeant Aden Jones joined me there that night and we rode in chairs the next day to river side. Stayed there all night and until 16:30 o'clock the next day waiting on Lieutenant Jack Manch. On Lieutenant Manch's arrival we loaded a small boat and travelled until night. Travelled by boat all the next day and part of the night arriving in Chuchow. Stayed two days in Chuchow.

'Went by train and bus to Hangyen which took four days. Took plane from Hangyen to Chungking.'

Above: Japanese officials examine the damage caused to a steel plant in Toyko, perhaps that hit by Lieutenant Gray's crew, in the aftermath of the Doolittle Raid.

Crew No.4
B-25 Mitchell #40-2282
Crew brought together as part of 95th Bombardment Squadron
Target Tokyo

Left to right: Lieutenant Harry C. McCool (navigator)
Corporal Bert M. Jordan (flight engineer/gunner)
Lieutenant Everett W. 'Brick' Holstrom (pilot)
Sergeant Robert J. Stephens (bombardier)
Lieutenant Lucian N. Youngblood (co-pilot)•••

The next away was Lieutenant 'Brick' Holstrom's B-25 40-2282, which lifted off three minutes after Gray's Mitchell at 08.33 hours.

'Proceeded in the direction of Tokyo but encountered severe fighter opposition,' wrote Doolittle of this aircraft. 'Endeavoured to get around the fighters and passed beyond Tokyo. They then decided to bomb a secondary target but were again attacked and driven off. Eventually dropped their bombs in the water and proceeded to a point near and Southeast of Shangjac where all crew members bailed out.'

The crew landed close together and were soon assembled. With the help of Chinese guerrillas, they were able to reach Chuchow.

Holstrom and his crew's flight was not quite as straightforward as Doolittle's report implied. The B-25's gun turret had jammed which meant that the aircraft's main defensive armament was practically useless. Potentially worse still, had been the news that there was a slow leak from one of their fuel tanks, and that the aircraft's compass was off by 15 degrees. When this was realised and their location determined, at which point they found themselves eighty miles north of Tokyo, it was calculated that they would have to fly 160 miles further than anticipated and with less fuel. The fighters which Doolittle referred to numbered six, but the Japanese defenders were not driven off because, of course, 40-2282's main guns were inoperative.

Holstrom later gave an account of the attack by the Japanese fighters, the Mitchell being at an altitude of only 75 feet as it approached Tokyo: 'Lucien Youngblood, my co-pilot, went back to transfer the last bit of gas from the bomb-bay to the wing tanks which did not quite fill the wing tanks up. He was still back there when I saw two pursuits coming at us and I immediately turned under them. One fired and I saw tracer bullets going over the pilots' compartment. I yelled to Youngblood to come back to his seat.

'The co-pilot then pointed out two more fighters going across our bow at about 1,500 feet and they looked as if they were ready to peel off on us. I told the navigator to tell Corporal Bob Stephens in the nose to try and use his guns. I had given him previous instructions to have the bombardier salvo the bombs if we were intercepted by pursuit, so the bombs were salvoed from about 75 feet.

'By this time we were indicating about 270 mph and I had turned under the two pursuits that had come across our bow and then turned due south. These pursuits all had non-retractable landing gear and I presumed them to be of the "97" type. McCool had come back to his compartment and said that he had seen several pursuits that looked like British Spitfires and by looking back through the navigator's side window I saw one of these planes on our right rear completing a firing pass. It had an in-line engine, retractable gear, and double tapered wings. I had no idea what type this was but supposed it was a Zero with an in-line engine. After running for about ten minutes nobody could see another airplane so I turned and headed down the coast of Japan towards China.'[7] Surprisingly, it seems, the fighters were unable to catch the bomber and the Japanese eventually gave up the chase.

The result of the faulty compass, as we have seen from Doolittle's report, meant that Holstrom and his crew could not reach Chuchow and had to bale out. Fortunately, all the men survived, but not after their fair share of adventures. The crewmen landed apart from each other, with Holstrom being captured by Chinese bandits who made him strip naked. Once they had taken all his possessions, his clothes, shoes and water canteen were returned to him.

His navigator, Harry McCool, landed safely on a mountain top. The next day, 19 April, was his twenty-fourth birthday, and he celebrated it with toffee candy and rainwater. That continued to be his sole diet for the following three days as he walked through continuous rainfall until he reached a local farm. There, he remembered fondly, he was treated to boiled, unhusked rice, and a poached goose egg sweetened with honey. He, and the rest of 40-2282's crew, lived to fight another day.

Crew No.5
B-25 Mitchell #40-2283
Crew brought together as part of 95th Bombardment Squadron
Target Tokyo

Left to right: Lieutenant Eugene F. McGurl (navigator)••
Captain David M. Jones (pilot)
Lieutenant Denver V. Truelove (bombardier)••
Lieutenant Ross R. Wilder (co-pilot)
Sergeant Joseph W. Manske (flight engineer/gunner)

As the pilot of the fifth Mitchell to get away, Captain David Jones took off, in #40-2283, at 08.37 hours.

Once again, Doolittle subsequently provided a brief account of Crew No.5's actions during the attack: 'Proceeded to Tokyo where bombing from 1200 feet, they made direct hits with three demolition bombs and one incendiary cluster on power stations, oil tanks, a large manufacturing plant and the congested area Southeast of the Imperial Palace. One factory bombed was a new building which covered approximately two city blocks. They then proceeded to China, baling out near and just Southeast of Chuchow. All crew members are safe.'

Below: The moment that a bomb dropped by one of B-25s explodes during the attack on 18 April 1942. It is not known which crew was involved. It is stated that eighty-seven were killed and nearly 500 wounded in the attack. (NARA)

Above: Gaining altitude, the B-25 banks away from scene of its exploding bomb, just out of view to the left of the image. (NARA)

Captain Jones' crew also made landfall to the north of Tokyo and had to head south until Tokyo Bay was spotted. This extra distance, plus the fact that the hurried take-off from *Hornet* had not allowed time to top up their fuel tanks, meant that they had less fuel than planned. Consequently, rather than spend valuable time trying to find his allocated targets, Jones decided to drop his payload on anything that looked suitable. This proved to be a wise decision as the bombs evidently caused considerable damage.

As with the other aircraft, the crew of 40-2283 encountered bad weather over China and had to fly on instruments and estimate their position above Chuchow before baling out. 'My bailout [*sic*] was a very frightening experience,' recalled Joe Manske. 'We were out of gas in closed-in weather conditions. I was first out of our ship and didn't realise how far each of us would be separated on the ground. After my 'chute opened, I panicked, being a small frame person, weighing about 110 pounds. With the weather socked in, I had nothing to compare my descent with. Being so light, I thought I was suspended and not falling.'[8]

Nevertheless, none of the men from #40-2283 were injured when they parachuted to the ground. Indeed, Jones and his four colleagues were the first crew to reach Chuhsien.

Crew No.6
B-25 Mitchell #40-2298
Crew brought together as part of 95th Bombardment Squadron
Target Tokyo

Left to right: Lieutenant Chase J. Nielsen (navigator)•
Lieutenant Dean E. Hallmark (pilot)++
Sergeant Donald E. Fitzmaurice (flight engineer/gunner)*
Lieutenant Robert J. Meder (co-pilot)**
Sergeant William J. Dieter (bombardier)*

Nicknamed *The Green Hornet*, the sixth B-25 away, at 08.40 hours, was that flown by Lieutenant Dean Hallmark. 'This plane landed in the Nangchang Area near Poyang Lake,' ran the words of Doolittle's 1942 account. 'From the best reports available (which are not to be relied upon) two crew members, presumably Sergeant Dieter and Corporal Fitzmaurice, are missing and three crew members, presumably Lieutenants Hallmark, Meder and Neilson, were captured by the Japanese. It was reported that one of these was bayoneted resisting capture but was not killed.'

Only one man from Hallmark's crew survived to tell the story of B-25 #40-229 – the navigator, Lieutenant Chase Neilson. He later recounted that having successfully bombed their targets in downtown Tokyo, they headed for China. They sighted land through the clouds and rain but their fuel ran out before they could reach the coast, and Hallmark, in what was described as 'an incredible display of steel nerves and skill' ditched the aircraft four miles from land.

Though Hallmark managed to land on the sea, the impact was so great he was catapulted through the aircraft's windshield, still strapped in his seat. Sergeant Dieter and Corporal Fitzmaurice were badly injured in the crash and drowned before reaching land.

Meanwhile, Dean Hallmark, Robert Meder and Chase Neilson had managed to swim to shore and found each other at daylight when they met up at the local Chinese garrison. They buried Dieter and Fitzmaurice on a small slope above the beach.

Following the raid on Tokyo, the Japanese immediately mounted a massive search through the eastern coastal provinces of China in search of any surviving airmen. For three days the three men evaded the Japanese patrols, but they were eventually overtaken by enemy forces in the small village of Shipuzhen, just off the coast of the East China Sea.

Hallmark was the first to be discovered late in the morning of 21 April, by an enemy patrol as the three officers hid in a hut. He stood up to reveal himself in the hope that the other two would not be spotted and, according to Neilson, Hallmark 'took one long, deep breath and refused to surrender his fellow officers'.[9]

Unfortunately, both Meder and Neilson were also discovered and, along with the crew of Lieutenant William Farrow's #40-2268, taken to the notorious Bridge House in Shanghai. This former hotel had been converted into a prisoner of war camp. There the raiders were beaten, tortured and placed on a starvation diet by the Kempeitai, the dreaded Japanese secret police.

For months the men suffered appalling treatment, with Hallmark losing 80lbs, being reduced to a mere skeleton and unable to stand. Finally, on 28 August 1942, the prisoners were subjected to a 'farcical' court martial. By this time, Hallmark was only semi-conscious, and he had to be carried into the courtroom on a stretcher. He was too weak to even brush the flies that gathered on his face. Because of his poor condition, he was separated from his comrades, who were transferred to the Civic Centre Prison in Shanghai, and taken back to Bridge House.

On 14 October 1942, Lieutenant Hallmark was transported to the Kiangwan prison compound in Shanghai, where he was informed that he was to be executed by firing squad the next day. On an overcast and foggy 15 October, Dean Hallmark and two other Doolittle raiders, Lieutenant Farrow and Sergeant Spatz, were taken to Shanghai Public Cemetery No.1. The men were given the opportunity to offer a silent prayer, before being blindfolded, forced to kneel and tied to a small cross. At 16.30 hours precisely, all three were shot in the head. Their bodies were subsequently cremated.

As stated earlier, only Lieutenant Neilson survived the ordeal of imprisonment at the hands of the Japanese. He was the only one of the Doolittle raiders who gave evidence to a War Crimes Commission after the war. In his testimony, he described one of the tortures meted out to the prisoners: 'I was given several types of torture ... I was given what they call the water cure ... I felt more or less like I was drowning, just gasping between life and death.'

The fifth member of the crew of #40-2298, co-pilot Robert Meder, died after months of malnutrition and mistreatment in solitary confinement in Nanking, his life ending in an unlit and infested cell measuring just 9 feet by 12 feet. His body was also cremated.

Following the Japanese surrender in 1945, the remains of Hallmark, Farrow and Spatz were recovered by members of the Allied War Crimes Commission and eventually taken back to the United States where, on 17 January 1949, they were laid to rest at Arlington National Cemetery.[10]

Above: A pictorial account of the Tokyo Raid and Doolittle's award of the Medal of Honor. (NARA)

Crew No.7
B-25 Mitchell #40-2261
Crew brought together as part of 95th Bombardment Squadron
Target Tokyo

Left to right: Lieutenant Charles L. McClure (navigator)
Lieutenant Ted W. Lawson (pilot)
Lieutenant Robert S. Clever (bombardier)••
Lieutenant Dean Davenport (co-pilot)
Sergeant David J. Thatcher (flight engineer/gunner)

As the raiders continued to launch themselves off the flight deck of USS *Hornet*, the next in line to get airborne, in the seventh position, was Lieutenant Ted Lawson's #40-2261. The time was 08.43 hours.

Lawson, however, only just about got airborne. In the excitement of the moment, Lawson forgot that his flaps were still retracted. So, without flaps, the Mitchell took off but dipped alarmingly as it left the carrier's deck. Lawson applied full power and the bomber, christened *The Ruptured Duck*, lifted away from the white-capped waves.

Doolittle's post-operation report reveals that Lawson's aircraft 'bombed the industrial section of Tokyo with 3 demolition bombs and one incendiary bomb. This aircraft landed in the water off the coast of China, west of Shangchow. One crew member was badly injured, three injured, one slightly injured. The badly injured crew member is thought to be Lieutenant Lawson, but we do not have definite confirmation of this. It is understood that he had a head and leg injury and it was necessary to give him several transfusions. Sergeant Thatcher was only slightly injured and it was due to his heroism that the lives of the other crew members were saved. Although badly cut on the head and knocked unconscious when the plane hit the sea and turned over, he nevertheless swam out into the perilous sea to secure the medical kit from the crushed plane. He was the only crew member physically able to carry on.

'After it became obvious that any further wait would result in capture by Japanese forces only 3 miles away, Chinese fishermen were persuaded by him to carry his injured crewmates to temporary safety around Japanese outposts. Then for three days Chinese fishermen were forced or persuaded by him to carry the injured crew members over difficult mountainous terrain until medical aid was reached.

'All of this plane's crew were saved from either capture or death as a result of Sergeant Thatcher's initiative and courage in assuming responsibility and tending the wounded day and night. As of the last report the 4 injured crew members, less Sergeant Thatcher who had proceeded on, had left the dangerous area with a Chinese escort and with Lieutenant T.R. White, of the Medical Corps from Aircraft No.40-2267 in attendance.'

It was later learned that as *The Ruptured Duck* sank, upside down, David Thatcher escaped through an emergency hatch. He was knocked unconscious, but only briefly. Lawson, Davenport and Clever, however, were hurled through the fuselage, receiving multiple injuries.

The five flyers were washed up onto Japanese-occupied territory, being found by Chinese fishermen who hid them in a hut. 'I bandaged everyone's wounds as best I could,' Thatcher told the military authorities in a report a month later. He said he had used the bandage in his first-aid kit to wrap Lieutenant Lawson's knee. 'I used my handkerchief on the cut on his arm,' he added. For the pilot's remaining wounds and those of the other crewmen, he said: 'I had to use old dirty rags that the fishermen gave us. I had no choice if I were going to stop their bleeding.'[11]

Helped by Chinese peasants and armed guerrillas, Thatcher took the four injured airmen on a gruelling five-day trek, by land and boat, to a hospital at Linhai on the mainland, carrying them on stretchers and sedan chairs, the whole time managing to evade Japanese troops. Though David Thatcher had saved the lives of his fellow crewmen, nothing could save Lawson's severely damaged leg, which had suffered a compound fracture and had to be amputated. This operation was carried out by Flight Surgeon Thomas White of Donald Smith's B-25, #40-2267, the crew of which made its way to the hospital at Linhai on 24 April. With only a limited amount of Novocain to act as an anaesthetic, White had to conduct the operation hurriedly. Even so, the anaesthetic wore off towards the end of the surgery.

The Americans left Linhai on 18 May as Japanese troops searching for the downed airmen moved into the region. For six days Lawson had to endure the swaying of a sedan chair over rugged terrain, and then an ancient un-sprung Ford station wagon, holding the stump of his leg above the floor of the vehicle as it bumped along the dirt roads.

When, on 24 May they reached Nanchang, they found that the Japanese had destroyed the airfield. As a result, the men were compelled to travel on, across rivers and over mountains, until they reached Hengyang where they were able to take a train to Kweilin. From there, at last, they were flown to Chungking via Kunming.

Right: One of two scrolls presented to General James H. Doolittle by Chu Chiu-jung, the mayor of the Chinese town of Heng-Yang, to mark the success of the attack on Tokyo. The two scrolls are known as the 'White Scroll' (seen here) and the 'Red Scroll'. The former was presented on behalf of the town's authorities, the latter on behalf of the mayor himself. The translation of the Chinese inscription reads: 'Commemorating the spreading of terror in the three islands [of Japan] by the brave general of the American air forces.' (NARA)

Crew No.8
B-25 Mitchell #40-2242
Crew brought together as part of 95th Bombardment Squadron
Target Tokyo

Left to right: Lieutenant Nolan A. Herndon (navigator)
Captain Edward J. York (pilot)
Staff Sergeant Theodore H. Laban (bombardier)
Lieutenant Robert G. Emmens (co-pilot)
Sergeant David W. Pohl (flight engineer/gunner). Aged 20, Pohl was the youngest man on the raid

Pulling back on the control column, Edward 'Ski' York's Mitchell, #40-2242, took off at 08.46 hours. 'This airplane bombed Tokyo with 3 demolition bombs and one incendiary bomb,' wrote Doolittle. 'Due to extremely high gasoline consumption they proceeded to Siberia landing at a point about 40 miles north of Vladivostok. All crew members o.k. and plane apparently saved. All were interned by the Russian Government and are now at Penza about 350 miles Southeast of Moscow.'

This crew had been hurriedly put together, as Lieutenant Robert Emmens explained: 'Ours was sort of a bastard crew made up of guys left over at Eglin flying on the B-25 that was a last-minute substitute for the one that bellied in the last day of training at Eglin. We formed as a crew after all the rest of the planes had left Eglin for the West Coast. We had never flown together before and had never made a practice take-off before the real one we made off the *Hornet*.'[12]

Everything had appeared to be going to plan at first for York and his crew until 135 minutes into their flight, when a check was taken on the fuel consumed by that time. They were staggered to find that they had used far more fuel than they should have done. They had no idea why this had happened, or whether or not they would continue to expend fuel at that rate.

That they were indeed using too much fuel was confirmed when York had to switch tanks forty-five minutes early, even before they had reached Japan. There was clearly no possibility of reaching China. The choice they faced was to bale out over the sea or make for the nearest non-enemy territory – the Soviet Union. Though Doolittle had not expressly forbidden the crews to land in the Soviet Union, he had made it plain that to do so might not be a good idea. The Soviets were not at war with Japan and if they treated the American flyers as allies, the political repercussions might be profound.

Over Japan, York's crew released their bombs on, they hoped, a power plant and a railway yard in a suburb of Tokyo, though they were unable to gauge how accurate or effective their bombing attempt had been. Then, taking a chance on the devil rather than the deep blue sea, they headed towards Vladivostok. After landing in Russia, the crew was held by the Soviets for thirteen months at various locations, before being moved to Ashkhabad, near the border with Persia. There they found a sympathetic Soviet officer who introduced them to an Afghan smuggler. The latter they paid the sum of $250 to lead them to the British embassy in Iran. The scheme worked and, with the help of British diplomats in Mashhad, all five men made their way to India and eventually back to the United States.

Below: Captain Edward York's B-25 pictured after its landing some forty miles north of Vladivostok on 18 April 1942. The aircraft was reportedly scrapped by Soviets sometime in the 1950s. (US Air Force)

Crew No.9
B-25 Mitchell #40-2303
Crew brought together as part of 34th Bombardment Squadron
Target Tokyo

Left to right: Lieutenant Thomas C. Griffin (navigator)
Lieutenant Harold F. Watson (pilot)
Technical Sergeant Eldred V. Scott (flight engineer/gunner)
Lieutenant James N. Parker Jr. (co-pilot)
Sergeant Wayne M. Bissell (bombardier)

At 08.50 hours, Harold Watsons' *Whirling Dervish* was the ninth aircraft away. Of this 'plane's part in the operation Doolittle wrote the following: 'Bombed Tokyo with 3 demolition bombs and one incendiary cluster, scored hit at Kawasaki truck and tank plant, another factory building and the congested industrial districts near the railroad station south of the Imperial Palace. The crew bailed out about 100 miles south of Poyang lake. All landed safely except Lieutenant Watson whose arm was caught in a parachute riser and dislocated at the shoulder. He suffered severe discomfort for a week until a doctor was encountered who put the arm back in place. When last seen about May 1 the arm was healing rapidly and Lieutenant Watson was experiencing no discomfort.'

Whirling Dervish encountered heavy anti-aircraft fire over Tokyo, but the crew, as Doolittle stated, had managed to release their bombs. Though they thought they had bombed the Kawasaki plant they in fact dropped all their four bombs on the Tokyo Gas and Electric Engineering Company.

Watson and his crew flew on to China through heavy cloud and rain, the storm continuing as they progressed inland. They flew deeper into China than any of the other Mitchells.

Above: Lieutenant General James H. Doolittle receives a commemorative plaque from Alexander T. Burton, of the North American Aircraft Co, at a Doolittle Raiders' reunion held in Miami Beach between 18 and 21 April 1947. The plaque was mounted with a piece of wreckage from one of the B-25s that took part in the attack – more specifically B-25 Mitchell #40-2303, *Whirling Dervish*, which was flown by Lieutenant Harold Watson's crew No.9. The plaque was subsequently presented to the Smithsonian Institute where it joined a number of similar objects. (NARA)

Lieutenant Tom Griffin later told of his experiences: 'With no visibility downward or upward, we had to trust entirely on our watches and our compass to guess at our approximate position. As navigator, I felt like excess baggage ... All hope of reaching our airfield destination was now lost because of the rough terrain, and lack of radio contact ... Our plane flew inland approximately 300 miles before we ran out of gas.'[13]

As the engines spluttered, the men knew they had to bale out. 'One by one we eased down (the bottom hatch) ... into nothing,' continued Griffin. 'Jumping at night and in a storm is an experience one will never forget. There were times during that descent from 10,000 feet when I thought I had missed the earth. The wind currents at the time must have been violent because I remember first being able to see my chute. It would be level with me and sort of fold up. Then it would swing up over my head, fill up, and come down on the other side once again spilling its air. However, it hung up on the tops of some bamboo trees, and I was lowered to earth with the greatest of ease ... I unbuckled my harness and moved off, leaving my chute ... above.'

The crew were arrested by Chinese soldiers and taken to the city of Ihwang. They eventually reached Chungking on 14 May.

Below: A close up of the relic from *Whirling Dervish* that was presented to Doolittle on the evening of 19 April 1947. Identified as part of the right engine nacelle, the piece of wreckage was recovered by the Rev. Charles L. Meeus, a missionary, who subsequently handed it to Bishop Paul Yu Pin, the Vicar Apostolic of Nanking, in Washington. In turn, Bishop Yu Pin presented it to Mrs Roosevelt, who suggested that it might prove of value in promoting war bond sales. The War Finance Division of the Treasury Department later presented it to the North American Aircraft Company. (NARA)

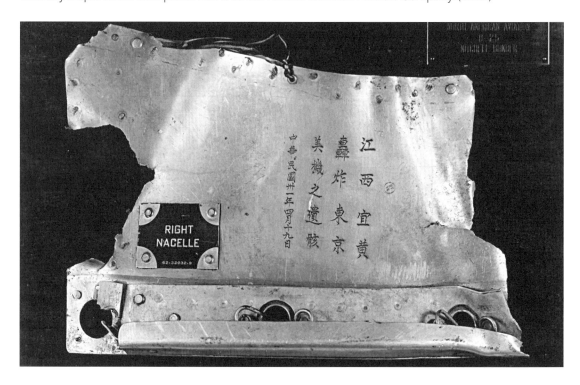

Crew No.10
B-25 Mitchell #40-2250
Crew brought together as part of 89th Reconnaissance Squadron
Target Tokyo

Left to right: Lieutenant Horace E. Crouch (navigator)
Lieutenant Richard O. Joyce (pilot); Staff Sergeant Edwin W. Horton Jr. (gunner)
Lieutenant J. Royden Stork (co-pilot); Sergeant George E. Larkin Jr. (flight engineer)••
The original USAF caption to this image states that Horton 'was substituted at the last moment
because of his knowledge of gun turrets – a constant source of trouble'

This aircraft was originally selected to take-off from USS *Hornet* two days after leaving California to test the B-25's ability to safely lift off. As already mentioned, that task was cancelled, and Joyce and his crew joined the raid to bomb the Japan Special Steel Company and other targets.

On the day of the operation, Richard Joyce's B-25 took off at 08.53 hours and, as Doolittle reported, the aircraft 'proceeded to Tokyo'. As his report notes, the crew 'bombed the Japanese Special Steel Company plants and warehouses in South Tokyo in the Shiba Ward 1½ miles north of Tana River with 3 demolition bombs and 1 incendiary cluster from 2500 feet. Proceeded to China and all crew members bailed out about 30 miles north of Chuchow. All o.k. (Jumped from 8000 feet).'

Joyce also submitted a report on his and his crew's part in the operation: 'We sailed from San Francisco and targets were assigned at sea, and maps, charts and target location, and all procedures, were studied constantly while at sea. The take-off was ordered at 7:30 A.M., April 18, 1942. An emergency since we were discovered by the Japanese 800 miles from Tokyo. We had hardly enough time to get courses and other data.

'The mission orders were to proceed to Tokyo to bomb our target; go back out to sea, proceed south around southern tip of island of Honshu hence to China; land at Chuchow, refuel; wait till dawn and favorable weather; take-off and fly to Chungking or if forced down, proceed to Chuchow and await orders.'

The crew of #40-2250 encountered broken cloud between 3,000 and 5,000 feet all the way from leaving USS *Hornet* until making landfall, then from landfall to the target the cloud thinned out to become scattered southwest of Tokyo. When Joyce was 100 miles from the Japanese capital the skies cleared completely, allowing 'unlimited' visibility.

As with the other raiders, Joyce had been ordered to approach the target below 1,500 feet. In his case, he flew over the sea at 500 feet, but rose to 3,000 feet when he reached land. He released his bombs at 2,500 feet. His primary target, as we have read, was the Japanese Special Steel Company plants and warehouses in south Tokyo, more specifically in Shiba Ward some 1½ miles north of the River Tana. His secondary target was given as being any part of the industrial area there, or military objectives in the vicinity.

According to his report, he scored a direct hit on the Japan Special Steel Company with two of his 500lb bombs, causing heavy damage. He dropped his other 500lb bomb on a 'thick' industrial area in Shiba. The incendiary cluster was unloaded over a dense industrial residential sector close to the Steel Company. The B-25 encountered heavy anti-aircraft fire and was attacked by nine Zero-type fighters at 5,000 feet, which Joyce evaded by diving below them, increasing the speed to 330mph after the bombs had been released. This was the only Mitchell to suffer any major damage over Japan, being hit once, resulting in an 8-inch hole being made in the fuselage just forward of the horizontal stabilizer.

As Joyce headed towards China, the weather closed in. 'On approaching the coast of China I encountered adverse weather conditions namely fog and rain,' he later recalled. 'I was forced to go on instruments about 100 miles from the China coast and remained on instruments until the time of leaving the ship. I had previously attempted to use my automatic flight control equipment, but it was not functioning properly and I had to fly the ship manually all the way.

'I made the trip from Tokyo to China at about 500 feet altitude and 1300 rpm and started at 29 inches of mercury and gradually reduced to 25 inches as my gas load reduced. I indicated about 160 to 165 mph. I picked up a strong tail wind across the China Sea which enabled me to go as far as I did. I held a course of 261 degrees true from the Ohsima Strait to China. About the time that my navigator estimated that I should begin to gain altitude for the mountains on the coast we were low enough to the water that we spotted an island and got a few glimpses of land as we came in over the coast.

'It was getting dark and still foggy and raining and getting worse. There was an overcast above us. We crossed the coast at about 20:40 o'clock ship time and I believe about 40 miles south of the entrance to Hangchow Bay. I climbed to 4000 feet over land and continued on course. I figured I had enough gas to just get me about as far as Chuchow and not much further. I figured my consumption roughly at about between 65 and 70 gallons per hour. I know it was less than 70 gallons per hour after leaving Tokyo. As we neared our ETA at Chuchow I realized that the weather was such that we could never expect to make a landing so I told the crew to get ready to bail out and I slowed the ship up to 125 MPH.

'I climbed to 9000 feet with about less than 15 minutes of gas left and told my rear gunner to jump which he did, we then released the escape door in the front when we were sure that it would not hit the rear gunner and the engineer-gunner, navigator, co-pilot and myself then jumped in that order. I rolled the stabilizer back to keep the ship from gaining too much speed and then I worked myself around to get out of the cockpit and had some trouble in squeezing between the armor plate back of the pilot and co-pilot seats and had to keep pushing the stick forward to keep the ship from stalling.

'I had little time to do anything after I got in position to jump. I gathered some food and equipment and jumped out through the escape hatch in the navigator's compartment where the rest of the crew had left except the rear gunner. I left the engines of the ship running. I dropped clear of the ship and pulled the rip cord and the chute opened and functioned perfectly except that the metal sheared on one of the leg strap buckles and the leg strap on my left leg parted and almost dropped me out of the chute. I slid down and the chest strap came up and smacked me in the chin with a stunning blow and at the same time jerked my pistol out of my shoulder holster and tossed it out into space. I was swinging quite badly and had some time to stop that but finally did. I estimate that I floated about one minute.

'I heard the plane below me and it hit the side of a mountain and exploded and burst into flame. A few seconds later I hit the ground which was quite a surprise to me. I was not very far from the airplane but I realized that I was on a pretty steep slope and could see very little for the fog and rain. I was uninjured. I got out of my chute and got my mussette bag [a widely-used item as an alternative to the standard issue backpack] and wrapped myself up in my parachute and tried to sleep and keep warm and dry.

'The next morning it was still foggy and when it cleared enough for me to see I started for the wreck of the plane. I had to go up over the mountain that I was on. I landed on top of a high mountain and on a steep slope with many boulders and cliffs. I realized that I was quite lucky that I was not seriously injured. The plane was only about a mile away but it took me four hours to get there.

'When I arrived at the scene of the crash which was also very high up in the mountains I found a number of Chinese there picking in the wreckage. I hailed them and made them understand that I was an American. They were very friendly. The plane had hit into the side of the mountain and sprayed over a large area and had burned. I was able to salvage nothing from it. It was a total loss. The Chinese farmers took me to a town that day and the next day I met some Chinese soldiers who took me to Tunki, Anhwei and eventually I made my way to Chuhsien, Chekiang. We abandoned the plane between 22:00 and 22:10 ship time. We flew for over 14 hours. I did not reach Tunki until four days later and Chuhsien a week later.'

Crew No.11
B-25 Mitchell #40-2249
Crew brought together as part of 89th Reconnaissance Squadron (crew members from
34th Bombardment Squadron)
Target Yokohama
Left to right they are: Lieutenant Frank A. Kappeler (navigator)
Captain Charles Ross Greening (pilot)
Sergeant Melvin J. Gardner (flight engineer/gunner)••
Lieutenant Kenneth E. Reddy (co-pilot)••
Staff Sergeant William L. Birch (bombardier)

At the controls of B-25 #40-2249, Captain Charles Greening took off at 08.56 hours. Doolittle's report on this aircraft, named *Hari Kari-er*, reads as follows: 'Proceeded to Yokohama and bombed oil refineries, docks, warehouses and industrial area of Yokohama with 4 incendiary clusters from 600 feet. After bombing proceeded to China abandoning ship at 10,000 feet at a point about 40 miles northwest of Chuchow. All crew members o.k.'

Greening's own account carries a little more detail than Doolittle's brief summary: 'Orders for take-off were given without warning. No last minute preparations such as weather data at target en route or destination were given. We were to report to Chuchow, China, as soon as possible if separated from ships …

'A large oil refinery and storage tank area was bombed with apparent complete success. Target used was camouflaged by roof tops to conceal work wherever possible. A large black column of smoke could be seen as result over 50 miles away.'

Greening also described the moments following the release of the bombs: 'When our bombs dropped, there were great sheets of flame and a terrific explosion that threw the copilot and me right out of our seats, even though we were belted, and banged our heads against the top of the cockpit … my mind was intent on my job, of course, but I remember that I also kept thinking, Oh, if my wife could see me now.'[14]

This was not, as Greening duly noted, the last of the action for his crew: 'Three small boats were attacked using .30 Cal nose gun. One boat burned. Estimated size 50 to 60 feet long … Several [enemy] flights were observed. Attack made only by four apparently Zero fighters with inline engines. 6 guns firing forward using either incendiaries or tracers. Hits were observed on right wing with no apparent damage other than dents in wing. Two pursuit were observed to be hit seriously enough to leave attack, one on fire. Neither were seen to crash. After bombs were released no difficulty was encountered in outrunning pursuit.'

As with others in the operation, rain and poor visibility were encountered as #40-2249 reached China. Greening continued down the Chinese coast at 3,000 feet, staying within the cloud to avoid detection and flying on instruments. When it was estimated that they were over Chuchow, the crew baled out, but at 9,000 feet, not the 10,000 given by Doolittle. The time was 22.00 hours.

Crew No.12
B-25 Mitchell #40-2278
Crew brought together as part of 37th Bombardment Squadron
Target Yokohama

Left to right: Lieutenant William R. Pound Jr. (navigator)
Lieutenant William M. Bower (pilot)
Staff Sergeant Omer A. Duquette (flight engineer/gunner)••
Lieutenant Thadd H. Blanton (co-pilot)
Technical Sergeant Waldo J. Bither (bombardier)

It was at 08.59 hours when the twelfth raider, *Fickle Finger*, took off from USS *Hornet*. Of its actions during the hours that followed, Doolittle later wrote: 'Proceeded to Yokohama and bombed oil refineries, tank farms and warehouses with 3 demolition bombs and 1 incendiary cluster from 1100 feet. Proceeded to China and all hands abandoned ship at a point about 40 miles northwest of Chuchow.'

What Doolittle failed to mention in this report is that, whilst en route to China, Bower's crew 'flew over a Japanese weather boat. They strafed and sank it before flying on.'[15]

In due course, Lieutenant William Bower also penned his own description: 'Take-off was ordered at 7:30 AM April 18, 1942 without sufficient warning to enable crew to gather necessary position, weather, etc., data. Individual orders were to report to Chuchow for gas, then proceed to Chungking or if forced to land elsewhere or otherwise hold at Chuchow for further orders …

'Heavy AA was encountered just prior to bomb release point from S, W, N, range was poor, elevation good. No hits were made on ship. After bomb release rapid descent to surface was made and AA was seen to score hits on barrage balloons causing their destruction. AA continued from rear and also from hill to the west until approximately two miles at sea. Bursts were of five, tracking excellent.

'Bombs were released in sequence on large warehouse, railroad siding at refinery and tank farm. Warehouse was seen to be hit and fired. Railroad tracks and tank cars also hit. Effect of last bomb and incendiary was not noticed due to heavy AA. Speed of run 200 m.p.h., altitude 1100 ft.

'One weather boat was sunk 100 miles east of Japan. No other attacks made by machine guns.

'No actual attack was made by enemy pursuit. Several biplanes evidently of obsolete type followed the plane at 1000 yds. for fifteen minutes but did not offer attack.'

Bower said that they encountered cloud over China which stretched from the surface to 11,500 feet. As with other aircraft, Bower had to fly on instruments. When it became evident that they would not be able to land at Chuchow, the crew assembled in the navigator's compartment and at 23.30 hours they all jumped from the doomed aircraft at five second intervals. Bower wss the last to leave after twenty seconds. They jumped at a height of 11,500 feet, with the B-25 on autopilot and the speed at 120 miles per hour.

'I landed on a mountain with no ill effects, wrapped up in the silk and slept till 5:30 AM,' continued Bower. 'Crew had been told to do likewise and await day before attempting to locate each other. The next morning I started down the mountain and walked east for several hours, then N.E. At a small village a school teacher was able to locate direction and distance of Chuchow. Walked SE till dark and slept until dawn.

'Three of the crew joined me at this village. The fourth joined us at noon the next day. Natives carried us to Sian where a car took us into Chuchow.

'Six nights were spent at Army Air station there and on Saturday evening we left by train for Yun San. A bus met us and in this we travelled three days to Heng Yang. A plane met us there and brought us to Chungking.'

Crew No.13
B-25 Mitchell #40-2247
Crew brought together as part of 37th Bombardment Squadron
Target Yokosuka

Left to right: Lieutenant Clayton J. Campbell (navigator)
Lieutenant Edgar E. McElroy (pilot)
Sergeant Adam R. Williams (flight engineer/gunner)
Lieutenant Richard A. Knobloch (co-pilot)
Master Sergeant Robert C. Bourgeois (bombardier)

Having been christened *The Avenger*, the thirteenth raider, Lieutenant McElroy's #40-2247, lifted off from the deck of USS *Hornet* at 09.01 hours. '[It] proceeded to the Yokosuka Navy Yard,' recounted Doolittlee, 'and bombed the dock area and one partially completed boat from 1500 feet with 3 demolition and one incendiary cluster. Bombs apparently had maximum effect, destroying everything on the dock and enveloping the boat in flames. Proceeded to China and landed near Poyang. Bailed out at 6,000 feet. All o.k.'

As was the case with many of his fellow pilots, Edgar McElroy also wrote his own mission report: 'Targets were assigned at sea and necessary maps, objective folders, etc. were furnished for study. Take-off order was given at 07:30 o'clock April 18, 1942, when 810 statute miles due east of Tokyo. Orders were to bomb target and proceed to Chuchow for refuelling and then proceed to Chungking. Carry no papers to identify origin of flight, destroy ship [aircraft] in case of forced landing in enemy territory and under no circumstances go to Russia …

'Take-off was accomplished at 0900 approximately 3 minutes after preceding ship. Take-off was very much like normal take-off. Capt. Greening who was our flight leader and Lieutenant Bower who was on his right wing were still in sight, so by using about 1475 rpm and about 29 inches, indicating about 170 mph, we were able to overtake them in about 30 minutes. We flew in formation with them on about 282 degrees (M) until landfall was made at about 1330. We had suspicioned for some time that we were too far north, so at about 1345 we took a course of about 250 degrees and reached land at about 1400.

'Immediately after crossing the coastline we decided we were still too far north so went back out to sea a safe distance from shore fire and started following the coast line. Later calculation showed that we had hit the coast about 50 miles too far north. We had seen no enemy aircraft and no very sizeable surface craft before we reached the coast except numerous small fishing boats.

'As we were following the coastline south, we saw about 4 freighters, apparently engaged in coastline shipping. At about 1420 we estimated that we were due east of our target, so we turned inland. Misjudging our position slightly, we came to an airfield on the southeast shore of Tokyo harbour, where we were fired upon with extreme inaccuracy. We immediately determined our position at this point and proceeded northeast to our target.

'We bombed our target exactly as planned, approaching from the east at about 1300 ft. and 200 mph indicated. Bombs were dropped in congested building area at about 1440 o'clock. The large crane was seen to be blown up and a ship in the building slips was seen to burst into flames. It is believed that all bombs fell in congested building and construction area. When some 30 miles to sea, we could see huge billows of black smoke rising from the target.'

From his vantage point in the bombardier's compartment, Master Sergeant Bob Bourgeois recalled looking down on Tokyo Bay and his targets: 'I could not believe my eyes. There they were, just like that Lieutenant Commander said. Aircraft carrier, tin cans, oil storage depots. It was something. They were right where he said they would be.'

McElroy's mission report went on to recount what happened next: 'We encountered no enemy aircraft but heavy AA fire over target was fairly accurate. We saw no barrage balloons. After bombing we immediately headed out to sea on a course of about 220 degrees. When well out to sea we turned southeast and headed for Yakashima islands, passing just to the south of these at about 1915.

'About halfway between our target and Yakashima we sighted a large submarine apparently at rest, and about 15 miles further on we sighted three large cruisers headed toward Japan. We ran in to instrument weather about 1½ hours short of the China coast, although it had been overcast since leaving Yakashima. At about 2100 we climbed to about 6,000 ft. We had flown a compass course of 260 degrees since leaving Yakashima. At 2230 we began preparing to bail out. Each man filled his canteen, put on his life vest, and filled a bag with rations, etc. All five men were assembled in the navigator's compartment. The ship was on A.F.C.E. We bailed out as close together as possible at 2245 so as to be together on the ground. I bailed out last, pulling the throttles all the way back before doing so.

Below: One of Doolittle's B-25s passes over the Yokosuka Naval Base and Naval Arsenal, south of Tokyo and Yokohama, on 18 April 1942. One source states that this picture was probably taken by a member of Lieutenant Edgar McElroy's crew No.13. (NARA)

'I did not go to the plane myself [after landing] but Sergeant Williams went to it and said it was completely burned up. Sergeant Williams received a wrenched knee when he hit a tree, but it was OK in a few days. Lieutenant Knobloch cut his hip when he bailed out, but it healed OK in a few days.

'The entire trip was made at 166 mph indicated, following the cruise chart accurately. We bailed out about 75 miles north of Poyane.

Below: Another view of Yokosuka Naval Base taken by one of the B-25s during the raid – though which crew was responsible it not known. Note the Japanese naval vessels in the foreground. (NARA)

'Lieutenant Knobloch and myself located each other about 0100 the next morning. Early the next morning we walked to the first village and after some difficulty with sign language they began leading us, as we later found out, toward soldiers. About 1000 o'clock as we were making a stop for some reason or another, we were joined by Lieutenant Campbell and Sergeant Bourgeois, and about 1100 o'clock we were joined by Sergeant Williams.

'The people kept taking us south and about noon we were met by the first soldier, who took us to the first garrison. All the people and soldiers were very kind to us and made every effort to make our journey to Chusien comfortable.'

The ship that McElroy saw burst into flames was the nearly completed light carrier *Ryūhō*. The damage to this vessel was such that her launch was delayed until November.

Above: Four of the Doolittle Raiders, all members of crew No.13, pictured with Chinese soldiers after their arrival on the Asiatic mainland following the raid. From left to right, the Americans are Lieutenant Campbell, Sergeant Williams, Lieutenant McElroy and Master Sergeant Bourgeois. (US Army)

Crew No.14
B-25 Mitchell #40-2297
Crew brought together as part of 89th Reconnaissance Squadron
Target Nagoya

Left to right: Lieutenant James H. Macia Jr. (navigator/ bombardier)
Major John A. Hilger (pilot)
Staff Sergeant Job Eierman (flight engineer)
Lieutenant Jack A. Sims (co-pilot)
Staff Sergeant Edwin V. Bain (gunner)••

Six minutes after Edgar McElroy's *The Avenger* had taken off, John Hilger's B-25 took to the skies at 09.07 hours. Doolittle wrote that Hilger 'proceeded to Negoya [*sic*] and bombed military barracks at Negoya Castle, oil storage warehouses northwest of the business district, military arsenal in the center of city and the Mitsubishi aircraft factory on the water front with 4 incendiary clusters from 1500 feet,' reported Doolittle. 'Proceeded to China and all crew members bailed out, landing southeast of and near Shangjoa.'

In time, Hilger submitted his own report on the mission: 'After sailing, all information was given out as to targets, routes, and probable time of attack. Take-off was ordered by the Naval

Above: Chinese soldiers and civilians accompany a group of Raiders whilst evading Japanese troops. To the right of centre, with his arm being supported, is Major John Hilger. By comparing this image with the pre-raid crew photograph, it would appear that the other US personnel present are, left to right, Lieutenant James Macia Jr., Lieutenant Jack Sims, and Staff Sergeant Job Eierman. (NARA)

Commander, however, ten hours prior to contemplated take-off due to interception of the naval force by an enemy sea craft. Take-off position was at Lat. 35°1 O N, Long. 153° 23' E. Due to suddenness of orders no weather data was available and no new instructions were given. Each pilot took off on his original orders to bomb his individual targets and proceed to Chuchow for fuel and thence to Chungking. Definite orders were issued not to go to Russia ...

'A course of 268° Magnetic was flown from the carrier and landfall was made near the cliffs south east of Tokyo. Course was then changed to parallel the coast until a point five miles off shore and south of Nagaya was reached.

Above: Two of the Raiders pictured with their Chinese helpers soon after 18 April 1942. Standing on the far left at the back is Major John Hilger, the pilot of crew No.14's B-25 #40-2297. The other survivor lying under the blanket in the left foreground is not identified in the original caption, but may well be Hilger's flight engineer, Staff Sergeant Job Eierman. (NARA)

'One enemy patrol plane (similar to B-26 in appearance) was encountered 600 miles east of Tokyo but it is believed he did not see our planes.

'The bombing attack was delivered at 15:20 (-10 zone time) and the targets attacked were (1) Military Barracks in Nagaya Castle Grounds, (2) Oil and Storage warehouse, (3) Military Arsenal, (4) Mitsuibishi Aircraft plant south of Nogaya. All the targets were the originally selected ones and all were squarely hit with incendiary clusters. Bombing approach was made at minimum altitude and bombs were dropped at 1500 feet and 200 m.p.h. Indicated. The rear gunner saw many small fires start and when we were thirty miles south on our way out and approximately 10 minutes after the bombing we could see a tall column of heavy black smoke over the city. I would estimate the height of the column to be 5000 feet and the mushroom head on the column would indicate very intense fires.

'After the bombing only one enemy plane was seen to take-off. It was a small monoplane but never attacked our ship and disappeared soon after it was sighted.

'The volume of A.A. fire was moderately heavy but accuracy was very poor. Only two or three shots were close enough to be uncomfortable. The size of the bursts indicated that the shells were of 37-40 mm in size. No machine gun fire was encountered. No barrage balloons were encountered.

'While over Japan our entire crew was impressed with the drabness of the cities and the difficulty of picking out targets. All buildings were grey and very much the same in appearance. The cities did not look at all the way we expected them to look from the information in our objective folders and on our maps.

'The maps which we used were misleading because the contour interval was too great. We had expected to make a very low approach from the sea into Nogaya but were forced up to almost 1000 feet at times by low hills which did not show on the charts.

'After the attack a course of 180° was flown until 15:45 at which time we were 20 miles off shore. Course was then changed to 225° and held until 16:00 at which time course was altered to 252°. The southern tip of Japan was passed at 19:18 and altered course to 262°.

'After leaving Nogaya six cruisers and one aircraft carrier were sighted. Three cruisers and one carrier were in one group and three cruisers were in another group. These two groups were about fifty miles apart off the south coast.

'About 300 miles off the China Coast we encountered rain squalls and lowering ceilings and about 100 miles off the coast at 20:15 the weather got so bad that we pulled up to 1000 feet and went on instruments. At 21:05 we estimated we should be over the coast line and started climbing to 7,000. We saw a few breaks but very few lights on the ground. At 22:20 we estimated we were over Chuchow and still on instruments. We had about 40 gallons of gas left and I changed altitude to 8,500 and ordered the crew to jump. The crew abandoned the ship quickly and with no confusion. After the co-pilot jumped I trimmed the ship for flight at 170 m.p.h. (A.F.C.E. Not operative) and abandoned ship.

'I heard the plane crash shortly after my chute opened and the site was later visited by the co-pilot. The ship was badly smashed and had been stripped by vandals.

'No injuries to crew members other than bruises and sprains.

'The entire route was flown at 100 feet, except when making the bombing runs and when on instruments near the China coast.

'Only a few of those who jumped managed to save any rations, etc. and it might be advisable to construct as an integral part of the parachute harness a pouch that will carry matches (waterproof), condensed ration and a sheaf knife. Each crew member carried a compass and very few of these were lost. The gun belts carried the gun, canteen, first aid packet and twenty rounds of ammunition. Only two of these were lost in jumping.

Above: Major John A. Hilger was Doolittle's second-in-command for the attack on 18 April 1942. Following the raid, Hilger returned to the China-Burma-India Theatre as a commander of a Bomb Group. (NARA)

'When I landed from my jump I was shaken up but not seriously injured. I was on a very steep mountain, so I made a tent of part of chute and rolled up in the rest of it and spent the night there. The next morning, I discovered a small village at the foot of the mountain and one of the villagers took me to a road where I met a military party out searching for us. I was taken to Kwang Feng, about 15 miles from where I landed and then sent to Chuchow the next night.'

Hilger was joined by the rest of his crew who all made it to Chungking without incident.

Above: Staff Sergeant Job Eierman pictured holding a parachute after the Raid prior to a flight from Mitchell Field, New York. After his return to the US, he was posted to a number of anti-submarine wings located on the East Coast of America until February 1945.(NARA)

Crew No.15
B-25 Mitchell #40-2267
Crew brought together as part of 34th Bombardment Squadron
Target Nagoya

Left to right: Lieutenant Howard A. Sessler (navigator/ bombardier)
Lieutenant Donald G. Smith (pilot)••
Lieutenant (Dr.) Thomas R. White (flight engineer)
Lieutenant Griffith P. Williams (co-pilot)
Sergeant Edward J. Saylor (gunner)

Lieutenant Donald Smith's bomber, B-25 #40-2267 which the crew had nicknamed *TNT*, lifted into the air at 09.15 hours. Doolittle's summary is as follows: 'Proceeded to Kobe and bombed the main industrial area, an aircraft factory, dock yards and yards in the north part of the Bay with 4 incendiary clusters, proceeded to China and landed in the water west of Sangchow. All crew members o.k.

'Lieutenant T.R. White, Medical Corps, a member of the crew, at great risk to his life and with exemplary courage remained inside the sinking ship [aircraft] with water rising dangerously until his surgical instruments and medical kit could be salvaged. The plane plunged down into 100 feet of water just after he had completed his effort and escaped. This action, together with his unselfish devotion to duty and attendance on the injured crew of airplane AC 40-2261 in spite of a Japanese advance into that area, indicated exemplary courage and deserves special commendation.'

Smith's targets were the Vyenoshita steel works and the Kawasaki aircraft factory. As they released their bombs, Smith and his crew spotted two enemy fighters racing towards them so they did not wait around to see the effects of their attack.

The reason that Smith had to 'ditch' his Mitchell off the Chinese coast was because as he flew inland both engines began to misfire and ahead of him was a range of mountains. Rather than take the risk of his engines failing as he tried to cross the heights, he decided to head back out to sea and crash-land on the water.

Upon reaching land on a small off-shore island, the crew found that they had been fortunate in reaching the only island in the area that was not garrisoned by the Japanese. The local Chinese promised to get the crew to Nandian Island and from there to the mainland.

Thomas White received the special commendation that Doolittle believed he had earned, being awarded the Distinguished Flying Cross along with the other Doolittle raiders.

Crew No.16
B-25 Mitchell #40-2268
Crew brought together as part of 34th Bombardment Squadron
Target Nagoya

Left to right: Lieutenant George Barr (navigator)•
Lieutenant William G. Farrow (pilot)++
Sergeant Harold A. Spatz (flight engineer/gunner)++
Lieutenant Robert L. Hite (co-pilot)•
Corporal Jacob DeShazer (bombardier)•

William Farrow's *Bat Out of Hell* was the last of the raiders to get away. The time was 09.19 hours. When Doolittle wrote the following report, his information was sparse: 'Landed on the Coast at Shipu south of Ningpo and crew was captured by soldiers of the puppet government. The best information available indicates that two crewmen are missing and three captured. Inasmuch as the two captured crews were in airplanes No. AC 40-2268 and 2298, it is possible that some confusion exists in the identification of these two airplanes and their location.'

Much has been learned since of the fate of this crew. The Mitchell ran out of fuel to the east of Nanchang and the five men successfully baled out. Shortly after landing, Farrow made contact with DeShazer, and the two men set off to walk, they hoped, to safety.

After a brief sleep in what they thought was a rice paddy, which daylight revealed was a graveyard on the edge of a village, they met their first Chinese. The villagers rather tentatively welcomed the strange visitors, unsure at first how the white men had arrived in their presence. Eventually, though, Farrow and DeShazer were able to explain their predicament and $200 of Farrow's emergency bribe money went the way of the village head man with the expectation that the flyers would be taken to Chungking.

The two men were fed and then taken to a hut where, to their dismay, the door was closed behind them and barred with a heavy beam. Only through the cracks in a small boarded window could they witness the unpleasant events that would enfold.

What they saw through that window was the appearance of a Japanese officer at the head of a company of soldiers. The officer shouted at the headman, who shook his head. The officer repeated himself, receiving the same negative response from the elderly Chinese. The officer did not ask a third time. He barked an instruction to two of his men, who promptly ran to one of the villagers and seized a large blanket. The soldiers knocked the headman to the ground and rolled him in the blanket. A third soldier then poured petrol over the blanket.

Farrow and DeShazer knew what was going to happen, and they could not let this brave man be burned to death on their behalf. They called out and hammered at the door of the hut. No one heard them.

They had to watch in horror as the officer struck a match and lit a small stick. This he handed to the headman's wife and told her to set fire to her husband. The terrified woman refused, so the officer grabbed her small son by the throat – and began to strangle the little child. Faced with a shocking choice between the murder of her husband or that of her son, the traumatized women threw the burning stick onto the blanket, which erupted in flame. The Japanese cheered at the chilling screams of the headman. Just to finish the job, after the fire had died down, two soldiers smashed in the skull of the dying headman with their rifle butts.[16]

There was no further resistance from the villagers, and the door to the hut was opened and Farrow and DeShazer became prisoners of his Imperial Majesty. As they were being dragged from the village, behind them they could hear the gunfire and the screams of the villagers as the Japanese ensured that there would be no one left to tell the tale of the American airmen.

Farrow and DeShazer were shortly to find that they were not the only raiders in the hands of the enemy, for they were taken, both blindfolded, to Nanchang where they were united with the rest of the crew of *Bat Out of Hell*. They had all been captured shortly after they had baled out.

As the men had feared, they were subject to interrogation. Farrow was the first, and when he refused to offer his interrogators anything other than name, rank and number, he was beaten.

Farrow was taken back to his cell. The next morning, 21 April, all five men were blindfolded and transported, by truck and then aeroplane, to Shanghai.

'We were put in solitary cells and forced to sit cross-legged on the floor,' recounted Lieutenant Robert Hite. 'I still had my heavy flight jacket on, but I shivered uncontrollably – probably from the cold but also because I was hungry and, I guess, scared.' What Hite also recalled was that when he was taken before a Japanese officer to be questioned, the officer already had a list of the eighty men who had taken part in the Doolittle Raid. Nevertheless, the five prisoners offered no further information to their interrogators, despite being told they would be shot if they did not cooperate.

At this point, the prisoners were flown to the place they had bombed, Tokyo. There they were handed over to the Kempeitai and incarcerated in the same prison as Lieutenant Dean Hallmark's crew – though neither group knew of the others' presence.

Below: A blind-folded Lieutenant Hite being led from a transport aircraft by his Japanese captors after he and seven other airmen had been flown from China to Tokyo. After about forty-five days in Japan, Hite, along with seven other Raiders, was taken back to China by ship and imprisoned in Shanghai. He was held for a total of some forty months before being liberated in 1945. His weight had dropped to 76lbs, from 180, by the time the war ended. (US Air Force)

Above: Robert Hite, in the centre, pictured with two other Doolittle Raid veterans late in 1945. Having been liberated by US troops on 20 August 1945, Hite remained on active duty until September 1947. He subsequently returned to active duty during the Korean War. (NARA)

During his first session with the Kempeitai interrogators, Farrow was subjected to what is now known as waterboarding – in which water was poured down his throat so that he could not breathe. When he passed out, he was allowed to regain consciousness before the treatment was repeated. But worse was to come. A tube was forced down his throat and water poured into it until his stomach was full and the water started to gurgle back up his throat. One of the guards then jumped up and down on his stomach. When this failed to elicit Farrow's cooperation, he was hung by his outstretched arms a few inches off the ground. He was left hanging in excruciating pain throughout the night.

What had perplexed the Japanese was how an aircraft as large as the B-25 had managed to take-off from an aircraft carrier. They desperately sought answers to such questions as the length of the carrier's flight deck, the number and weight of the bombs each Mitchell carried, and the number of aircraft and crew involved. Potentially, the entire war planning of the Japanese had been thrown into jeopardy if the United States armed forces could strike at Tokyo from their carriers in this manner.

When the Japanese attacked Pearl Harbor they knew that all the US carriers were not present but had continued with their attack regardless. They had regarded the American battleships as the greatest threat to their ambitions – but if the Americans could launch medium bombers anywhere throughout the Pacific, the entire Japanese war plan was in danger. The tough American flyers refused to give the enemy the answers they sought, and with every refusal to speak came harsher punishment –and with it the constant threat of worse to come if they did not comply.

The next day, the torture continued, with the men being forced to kneel with large bamboo joints pushed behind their knees. This was painful enough in itself, but then the sadistic guards would jump on their thighs, forcing the knee joints to spread. The pain was so excruciating that the men almost passed out. Another dreadful act undertaken by the interrogators was the binding of the fingers of the hand and then driving a stick between each pair of fingers. One of the torturers would squeeze the fingers together while another pushed sticks backwards and forwards between the bound and squeezed fingers. This bizarre treatment, as well as causing intense pain, frequently caused fractures to the fingers.[17]

One particular theme ran through all the interrogations – the insistence that the men admitted that they had targeted civilians, which would enable the Japanese authorities to declare that the American flyers were war criminals. This, it was later learned, was to help the senior Japanese generals save face for having allowed Tokyo to be attacked.

Refusing to acknowledge that they had intentionally attacked hospitals and schools, as the Japanese claimed, inevitably meant more torture. This included repeatedly pushing sharpened bamboo sticks through the skin between Farrow's fingers. When this did not work, Farrow was told he was to be summarily executed, and a mock execution took place with the blindfolded young lieutenant convinced he was about to die.

For eighteen days and nights, the crews of both #40-2268 and #40-2298 were tortured until, on 22 May, the men were presented with written confessions. These they were ordered to sign or face execution. After signing the false confessions, the torture stopped.

The prisoners were taken by ship to Shanghai and, as we have already read, placed in the Bridge House jail before Farrow, Spatz and Dean Hallmark, were executed on 15 October 1944.

The other captured airmen remained in military confinement on a starvation diet, their health rapidly deteriorating until April 1943, when they were moved to Nanking. There they began to receive slightly better treatment, but Lieutenant Bob Meder developed beriberi and died on 1 December 1943. The survivors were finally liberated by US troops in August 1945.

Above: Robert L. Hite. At the time of Hite's death on 29 March 2015, aged 95, only two of the other Raiders were still alive, Richard Cole and David Thatcher. In his obituary in the *New York Times*, it was noted how Hite 'had volunteered for it [the attack] and was assigned to pilot one of its B-25 bombers, but was bumped from the roster when all the planes originally massed for the raid could not fit on the aircraft carrier *Hornet*, which was to ferry them toward their target. At the last minute he replaced the co-pilot of another crew. He was 22.' (NARA)

PART THREE

The Aftermath

CHAPTER 4

War Crimes

There had to be some form of accountability for the treatment the prisoners endured at the hands of the Japanese and for the three executions. On 27 February 1946, the United States Military Commission, sitting at Shanghai, tried Lieutenant General Shigeru Sawada, Second Lieutenant Okada Ryuhei and Lieutenant Wako Yusei for being members of a Japanese Military Tribunal, which, 'did at Kiangwan Military Prison, Shanghai, China, knowingly, unlawfully and wilfully try, prosecute and adjudge eight members of the United States forces to be put to death in violation of the laws and customs of war'. At the same time, Tatsuta Sotojiro, Captain in the Japanese Imperial 13th Expeditionary Army in China, was accused of causing the deaths of the three airmen.

A statement of the crimes these individuals had committed read as follows: 'On 28th August, 1942, after spending approximately seventy further days at the Bridge House Jail, Shanghai, in small verminous and insanitary cells, all eight fliers were removed to the Kiangwan Military Prison, on the outskirts of Shanghai. At the time of their transfer, all the fliers were weak and under-weight and one was very ill. On arriving, they were assembled in a room before several Japanese officers, who, they later learned, constituted their court-martial.

'The accused Wako and Okado were among the members of the court. The accused Tatsuta attended the trial voluntarily and not officially, as a spectator, for a short time. The fliers stood

Above: Lieutenant Chase J. Nielsen. The sole survivor from his crew, No.6, Nielsen was the only Doolittle Raider to give evidence at the War Crimes trials. (NARA)

before the Japanese officers who conversed in their own language. The sick prisoner was carried in on a stretcher where he continued to lie during the proceedings. He was ill but was not attended by a doctor or a nurse. He did not, by his eyes or facial expression, appear to recognize the others; nor did he make any statements.

'The fliers were asked a few questions about their life histories, their schooling and training. After they answered, one of the Japanese stood up and read from a manuscript in Japanese. The fliers made no other statement. There was an interpreter present, but he did not interpret anything except the fliers' names and ranks, and similar details.

'The proceedings lasted about two hours at the very most. The fliers were not told that they were being tried; they were not advised of any charges against them; they were not given any opportunity to plea … No witnesses appeared at the proceedings; the fliers themselves did not see any of the statements utilized by the court that they had previously made at Tokyo. They were not represented by counsel; no reporter was present; and to their knowledge no evidence was presented against them.'

There were other accusations of ill-treatment of the prisoners after the executions which were also read out before the Commission.

The Commission determined that as for Shigeru Sawada, although he was the Commanding General of the 13th Japanese Army, he was absent at the front and had no knowledge of the trial until his return to Shanghai three weeks after the results of the trial. It was found that although he did not make strong written protests to Imperial Headquarters in Tokyo, he did make oral protest to his immediate superior, the Commanding General of the Japanese Imperial Expeditionary Forces in China, to the effect that in his opinion the sentences were too severe.

The Commission decided that while he was negligent in not personally investigating the treatment being given to the American prisoners, he was informed by his responsible staff that they were being given the treatment accorded Japanese officer prisoners. He was sentenced to five years' hard labour.

Wako Yusei was a judge at the trial of the American airmen and, although he was legally trained, he accepted the evidence without question and tried and 'adjudged the prisoners on this evidence which was false and fraudulent'. However, he voted for the death penalty only because he was following 'special' instructions from his superiors. He was sentenced to nine years' hard labour.

By contrast, it was determined that Ryuhei Okada, although he sat as a judge at the trial, had not received any instructions from his superiors and enjoyed freedom of conscience in determining as to the guilt or innocence. However, Okada had no legal training and did protest about his unsuitability to sit on any tribunal. He was sentenced to five years' hard labour.

These sentences may seem surprisingly lenient, but none of the above men did the killing – that was left to Sotojiro Tatsuta. Naturally, one might assume that the Commission would have no option but to order the death sentence for Tatsuta. Remarkably, the Commission found that Tatsuta carried out the executions merely as part of his official duties as prison warden. He was sentenced to five years' hard labour.

Astonishingly, despite Lieutenant Neilson's graphic personal testimony as to the appalling and brutal treatment some of the Doolittle Raiders received, none of the defendants were charged with responsibility for torturing the prisoners.[18]

CHAPTER 5

The Post-Raid Assessment

Above: A number of the Raiders are borne to safety by their Chinese rescuers. Of the eighty men who left *Hornet* on 18 April 1942, sixty-four eventually returned home. (NARA)

The first the American public knew of the raid was in the newspapers the following day, 19 April. In some cases, the U.S. press quoted information gleaned from their Japanese counterparts, the following appearing in *The New York Times*: 'Enemy bombers appeared over Tokyo for the first time in the current war, inflicting damage on schools and hospitals. Invading planes failed to cause any damage on military establishments, although casualties in the schools and hospitals were as yet unknown.

Above: According to the original caption, this group of 'bewildered Chinese natives of a village near where [a] bomber crashed [are] seeing their first white man'. (NARA)

Opposite page: Survivors of the Raid are grouped outside a shelter carved from the mountainside. The original caption states that 'they lived there for 10 days after assembling from their Chinese Mountain retreats. Jap planes raided nearby villages frequently.' (NARA)

'This inhuman attack on these cultural establishments and on residential districts is causing widespread indignation among the populace ... Nine of the attacking planes were shot down and the rest repulsed by heavy anti-aircraft fire.'

A slightly later, and much exaggerated, Japanese report gave a few more details: 'A large fleet of heavy bombers appeared over Tokyo this noon and caused much damage to non-military objectives and some damage to factories. The known death toll is between three and four thousand so far. No planes were reported shot down over Tokyo. Osaka was also bombed. Tokyo reports several large fires burning.'[19]

Though these reports indicated that the raid had succeeded, it was not until a message was received on 20 April from General Joseph Stilwell, who was the Allied chief-of-staff to the Chinese leader Chiang Kai-shek, that the fate of the crews and their aircraft was learned: 'Chinese air force has confused message in substance as follows: 3 repeat 3 crew members report they flew 21 hours,

Above: Parasol carrying members of the Chinese Army search for any pieces of wreckage or items of interest from one of the B-25s whose crew had baled out. (NARA)

that 16 airplanes started, that bad weather dispersed the formation. Weather still precludes flying in entire area. Further information will be forwarded when received.'[20]

Later that same day, the Chinese Minister for Foreign Affairs sent a note he had received from Doolittle to 'Hap' Arnold. This differed slightly from that recalled by Doolittle himself: 'Mission to bomb Tokyo has been accomplished. On entering China we ran into bad weather and it is feared that all planes crashed. Up to the present already five crews are safe.[21]

The White House, though, remained tight-lipped. No official announcement was forthcoming until 21 April. At a press conference in the Executive Office, the president was asked about the raid, to which question Roosevelt, determined that the Japanese would learn nothing from his comments, answered, to the amusement of the assembled reporters, that the attack had been delivered 'from our new secret base at Shangri-La!'

Roosevelt was privately delighted with the raid. He wrote to Winston Churchill: 'As you will have seen in the press we have had a good crack at Japan by air and I am hoping that we can make it very difficult for them to keep too many of the big ships in the Indian Ocean [thus helping Britain in its defence of India]. I am frank to say that I feel better about the war than at any time in the past two years.'[22]

On the other hand, the available information that reached the US in the aftermath of the raid was not universally well received by the military. While 'Bull' Halsey called the raid 'one of the most courageous deeds in all military history', Arnold declared the following: 'From the viewpoint of an Air Force operation the raid was not a success, for no raid is a success in which losses exceed ten per cent and it now appears that probably all of the airplanes were lost.' Despite this view, Doolittle was immediately promoted to the rank of brigadier general and was awarded the Medal of Honor.

All the other crew members received the Distinguished Flying Cross, twenty-three of which were distributed at a ceremony held at Bolling Field airbase, in Washington D.C., on 27 June 1942. Up until this time, those twenty-three raiders who had made it home had been ordered to remain silent about the attack: 'You will grant no interviews with the press nor pose for photos and in your communications to your home [you] will advise them simply that you are back in the United States. Use the utmost caution until such time as you have been given a directive … on what you can say and do, so as not to jeopardize the security of others going into the field. In other words, be most cautious with everyone except authorized intelligence officers of the United States Army.'[23]

After the raid, the Army Air Forces' Director of Intelligence Service produced an Informational Intelligence Summary which drew the following conclusions: 'Sixteen B-25s made the flight to Japan. From the pilots or crew members of thirteen of these planes have come reports from which a reasonable estimation of the execution and success of the mission may be made.

'The preparation was thorough. The flight was well executed and, in most cases, primary targets were reached, hits were made at low altitudes, and explosions, followed by smoke and fires, were observed by several ships as they passed over the area.

'The magnitude of the destruction and the effect on Japanese morale may not be evaluated from the few rumors [sic] that have come out of the enemy's country. Had it been known beforehand how complete was going to be the surprise and how weak the resistance, it would have been possible to concentrate all planes on such a target as the Mitsubishi Aircraft Factory.

'The reaction on our Allies and the American public was essentially favorable. Any encouragement, however, accruing to the Chinese must have been tempered by the fact that immediately following the raid the Japanese initiated a severe attack on those areas in China which they suspected had been used in the project.'

Doolittle also provided his assessment of the raid: 'In almost every case primary targets were bombed. The damage done far exceeded our most optimistic expectations. The high degree of damage resulted from the highly inflammable nature of Japanese construction, the low altitude from which the bombing was carried out, and the perfectly clear weather over Tokyo, and the careful and continuous study of charts and target areas.

'Inasmuch as messages must have been received at some message center, we can only presume poor dissemination of information or the complete failure of their communication system.

'As previously mentioned, the take-off occurred almost ten hours early due to contact being made with enemy surface craft. In addition to this, the take-off was made on the 18th instead of the 19th as originally planned and agreed due to the Navy getting one day ahead of schedule and the undesirability of remaining longer than necessary in dangerous waters.

'We had requested a fast run-in at night and slow day progress in order that we might be within safe distance of Tokyo at any time during the take-off day. This was not expedient from a Navy viewpoint due to their poor manoeuvrability at slow speeds and the undesirability of running in any closer than was absolutely necessary.

'We appreciated the desirability of advising Chungking of our premature take-off but due to the necessity of strict radio silence, this could not be done prior to our actual take-off. We requested that Chungking be advised immediately after we took off and felt that even though they were not advised by the Navy radio that the Japanese radio would give them the desired information.

'As a matter of actual fact, Chungking did know that we were coming but official information was not sent to Chuchow, presumably due to the extremely bad weather and the communication difficulties resulting therefrom. As a result of this, no radio homing facilities were provided for us at Chuchow, nor were light beacons or landing flares provided. To the contrary, when our planes were heard overhead an air raid warning alarm was sounded and lights were turned off. This, together with the very unfavorable flight weather over the China Coast, made safe

Right: USS *Hornet* arrives at Pearl Harbor, after the Doolittle Raid, on 30 April 1942. Two US Navy PT boats (short for Patrol Torpedo boat), PT-28 and PT-29, are pictured speeding by in the foreground. (USNHHC)

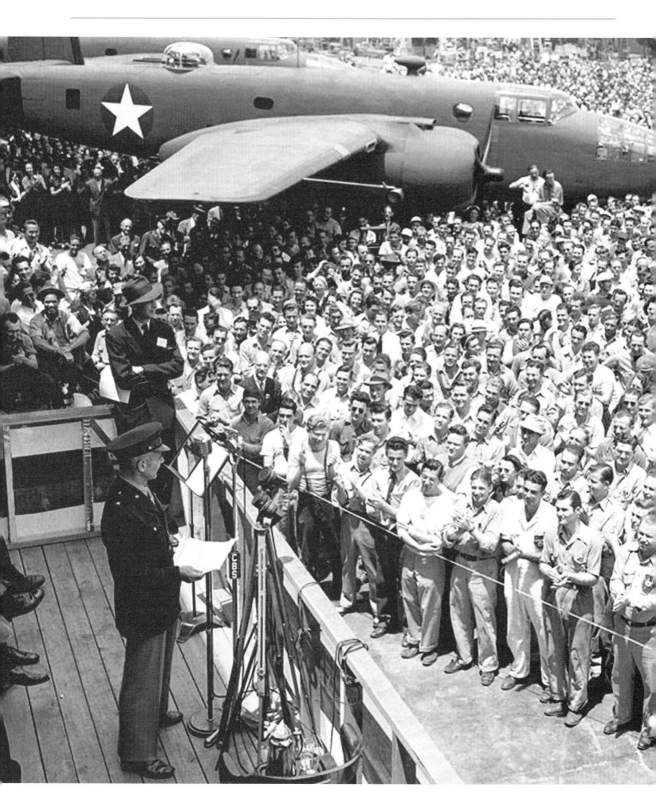

landing at destination impossible. As a result, all planes either landed either near the Coast or the crews bailed out with their parachutes.

'Before leaving China, arrangements were made with General Koo Chow Tung and Madam Chiang Kai-shek to endeavor to ransom the prisoners who had fallen into the hands of the puppet government. Some consideration was given to attempting the rescue of the prisoners that had fallen into Japanese hands in the vicinity of Payang Lake but it was indicated, due to the strong Japanese position, that at least two regiments would be required and that the chance of the prisoners being killed during the action was so great that the idea was abandoned. Negotiations were being carried on, when the writer left China, to the end of offering small guerrilla bands a certain amount of money for each prisoner that they could bring out of Japanese occupied territory alive.'

The Japanese response to the raid was beyond anything that Doolittle or his superiors could ever have imagined. As the Director of Intelligence Service mentioned, it was the Chinese in the areas that helped the American flyers who paid the heaviest price. Reports of murders, torture and rape on an almost unimaginable scale, conducted with utter merciless brutality on a helpless people, were numerous. While the exact number of people killed by revengeful Japanese is not known, it is certain that thousands, possibly as many as 250,000, Chinese lost their lives during the Japanese reprisals. Chuchow – Doolittle's intended destination – was the subject of repeated bombing attacks by the Japanese which resulted in the death of 10,246 people and left another 27,456 destitute.[24]

Left: Lieutenant Colonel James Doolittle addresses a throng of aircraft workers at the North American Aircraft Co. plant on 1 June 1942. (NARA)

Opposite page: An Office of War Information portrait of Brigadier General James H. Doolittle. Doolittle had been promoted by two grades, to Brigadier General, on the day after the Tokyo attack, bypassing the rank of full colonel. (NARA)

Below: Brigadier General James H. Doolittle receiving the Medal of Honor from President Franklin D. Roosevelt for his part in the Raid. Looking on, left to right, are Lieutenant General H.H. Arnold, Chief of Army Air Forces, Mrs. Doolittle, and then Chief of Staff, General George C. Marshall. The citation, dated 9 June 1942, states: 'For conspicuous leadership above the call of duty, involving personal valor and intrepidity at an extreme hazard to life. With the apparent certainty of being forced to land in enemy territory or to perish at sea, Gen. Doolittle personally led a squadron of Army bombers, manned by volunteer crews, in a highly destructive raid on the Japanese mainland.' (US National Museum of the US Navy)

There was also another, equally unexpected, response to the raid by the Japanese. They had failed to sink any of the Pacific Fleet's aircraft carriers in the attack upon Pearl Harbor, and the consequences of that became all too apparent when the B-25s appeared over Tokyo. It was self-evident that if Japan was to maintain its dominance in the Pacific, the American carriers would have to be eliminated.

This led to the Japanese Naval General Staff agreeing to Admiral Yamamoto Isoroku's plan to draw the US Navy's carrier fleet into a general action, by attacking America's outermost base at Midway Island. The Pacific Fleet, however, was lying in wait and it was Yamamoto's carriers that were destroyed, turning the War in the Pacific decisively in favour of the Allies.

Above: A group photograph of some of the Doolittle Raiders who had gathered in Washington D.C. on 18 June 1942. In the front row, left to right, are: Major John Hilger (crew No.14); Captain Charles Greening (crew No.11); Lieutenant (Dr.) Thomas White (crew No.15); and Lieutenant Donald Smith (crew No.15). Standing behind them, also left to right, are: Lieutenant Dean Davenport (crew No.7); Lieutenant William Pound Jr. (crew No.12); Lieutenant William Bower (crew No.12); Lieutenant James Macia Jr. (crew No.14); and Lieutenant Denver Truelove (crew No.5). (NARA)

This was conceded by the lead pilot of the attack upon Pearl Harbor, Fuchida Mitsuo: 'Headquarters spokesmen sarcastically pooh-poohed the attack as not even a "do-little" but rather a "do-nothing" raid. In point of physical damage inflicted it was true that the raid did not accomplish a great deal.

'But the same could not be said of its impact on the minds of Japan's naval leaders and its consequent influence on the course of the war at sea. The fighting services, especially, were imbued with the idea that their foremost duty was to protect the Emperor from danger. Naturally they felt that it would be a grave dereliction of this duty if the Emperor's safety were jeopardized by even a single enemy raid on Tokyo.'[25]

Above: On 8 July 1942, Lieutenant Ted W. Lawson was decorated with the Distinguished Flying Cross whilst undergoing treatment at Walter Reed Hospital, Washington D.C. It was described as the 'first such ceremony conducted at the Army Medical Center during this world war'. Shown with him here are his wife, Ellen Arlene Lawson, and Secretary of the Treasury Henry Morgenthau Jr. Speaking to reporters at the time, Lawson remarked that 'I don't want a soft job on somebody's shelf. I think I can do the Army some good in aeronautical engineering.' (NARA)

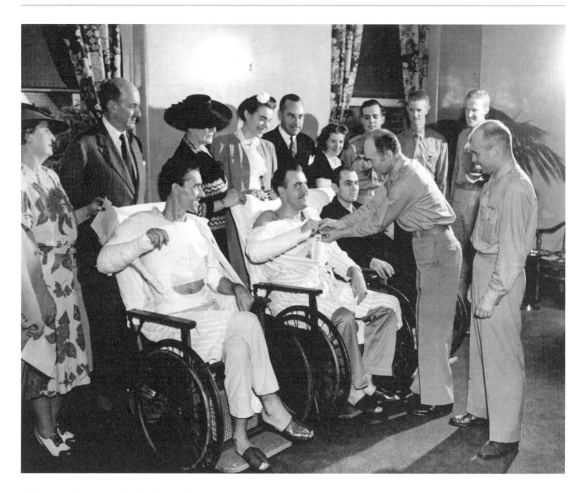

Above: Photographed during the same ceremony on 8 July 1942, Major General Millard F. Harmon, Chief of the Air Staff of the Army Air Forces, pins the Distinguished Flying Cross to Lieutenant Harold Watson. Doolittle is standing behind Harmon. To Watson's right is Lieutenant Charles McClure who was similarly decorated. McClure would be hospitalized until June 1943. (NARA)

Opposite page top: During his visit to the Walter Reed Hospital, Major General Chu Shih-Ming took the opportunity to present Lieutenant Charles L. McClure, sitting on the left, Captain Harold F. Watson, seated in the centre, and Lieutenant Ted W. Lawson, on the right, with the Military Order of China. The women in the background, are, again left to right, Mrs R.D. McClure (Charles' mother), Miss LaVerne Rosegrant (Charles' fiancée), Mrs Watson, and Mrs Lawson. Brigadier General James H. Doolittle is standing behind Lieutenant Ted W. Lawson. (NARA)

Opposite page bottom: Whilst at the Walter Reed Hospital, Washington D.C., three of the Raiders spread out a map of Japan to show Major General Chu Shih-Ming (on the far right), the Military Attaché at the Chinese Embassy, their objectives in the attack on 18 April 1942. The three raiders are, from the left, Captain Harold F. Watson, Lieutenant Ted W. Lawson, and Lieutenant Charles L. McClure. The picture was taken on 25 July 1942. (NARA)

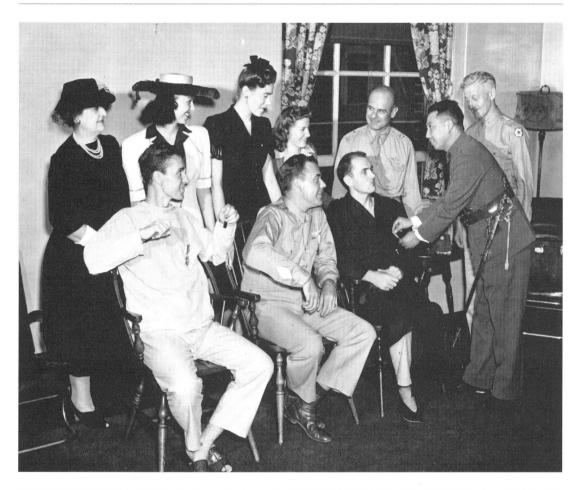

Left: Doolittle Raiders lined up at Bolling Field to be decorated by Lieutenant General Henry H. 'Hap' Arnold on 27 June 1942. Note the Douglas B-18 Bolo medium bombers in the background. (NARA)

Below: Lieutenant General 'Hap' Arnold, on the left, in discussion with Brigadier General James H. Doolittle during the ceremony at Bolling Field. One member of the crowd watching from the grandstand that day was a young schoolboy by the name of Samuel 'Murt' Guild Jr., who, was present by virtue of the fact that his father was stationed at Bolling Field at the time. Guild Jr. would subsequently become a candidate to serve as an astronaut for NASA. The ceremony had a profound effect on the young Guild: 'It was one of those things one doesn't forget and probably helped attract me to the newly organized Air Force.' (NARA)

Above: Lieutenant General Henry H. Arnold pins a medal on Captain Travis Hoover, crew No.2's pilot, with Lieutenant William Bower, the pilot of crew No.12, waiting his turn at Bolling Field. (NARA)

Opposite page top: For their actions during the attack, a number of the Doolittle Raiders were decorated by the Chinese at Chungking, China, on 29 June 1942. The investiture was performed by Madame Chiang Kai-shek, seen here with some of the raiders and other Chinese officials. A Chinese political figure also known as Soong Mei-ling or Soong May-ling, Madame Chiang Kai-shek was, at the time, the First Lady of the Republic of China, the wife of Generalissimo and President Chiang Kai-shek. The following series of photographs were taken during the ceremony. (NARA)

Opposite page bottom: An almost identical view to that in the previous photograph. The caption states that the individuals in this shot are, left to right: Lieutenant Frank Kappeler; Captain Charles Greening; Lieutenant Kenneth Reddy; Madame Chiang Kai-shek; Lieutenant Lucian Youngblood; Lieutenant Eugene McGurl; Lieutenant Jacob Manch; and Lieutenant Ross Wilder. (National Museum of the US Navy)

Above: Some of the officers line up for the awards to be presented from Madame Chiang Kai-shek. To the left of her can be seen Doolittle, Major John Hilger and Lieutenant Richard Cole. (NARA)

Below: Madame Chiang Kai-shek is shaking hands with Lieutenant Clayton Campbell, the navigator on crew No.13. To Campbell's immediate right is the co-pilot of his crew, Lieutenant Richard Knobloch, whilst beyond him is Lieutenant J. Royden Stork, the co-pilot on crew No.10. (NARA)

Above: Lieutenant Horace E. Crouch, the navigator on B-25 Mitchell #40-2250 which was flown by crew No.10, is invested by Madame Chiang Kai-shek. (NARA)

Left: It is Major John Hilger's turn to be decorated. Doolittle can be seen standing just behind him. (NARA)

143

Above: The ceremony continues on 29 June 1942. Left to right in this photograph are: Major John Hilger; Doolittle himself; Madame Chiang Kai-shek; Lieutenant Richard Cole; Lieutenant Henry Potter; Lieutenant Edgar E. McElroy, shaking hands with Madame Chiang Kai-shek; Lieutenant Richard Joyce; and Lieutenant Jack Sims. (NARA)

Below: Madame Chiang Kai-shek pins an award to Lieutenant Henry Potter's chest. Behind them is Major John Hilger, whilst Lieutenant Edgar McElroy is standing on the right awaiting his turn to be invested. (NARA)

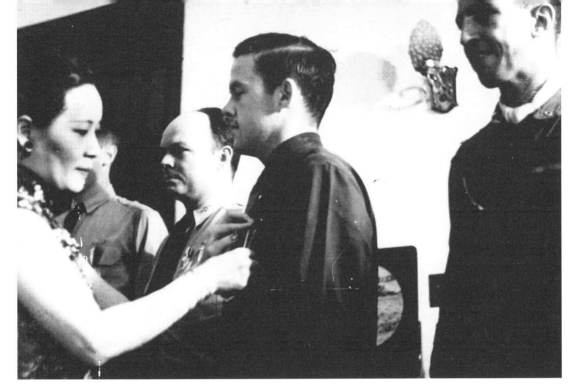

Above: Madame Chiang Kai-shek continues in her task of honouring the Doolittle Raiders. With Lieutenant Henry Potter (just visible) and Lieutenant Edgar McElroy in the background, a medal is pinned to the chest of Lieutenant Richard Joyce. Lieutenant Jack Sims is awaiting his moment of glory. (NARA)

Below: Taken moments after the previous image, Lieutenant Jack Sims is invested by Madame Chiang Kai-shek. To the left of him is Lieutenant Richard Joyce, and on the far-right Lieutenant J. Royden Stork. (NARA)

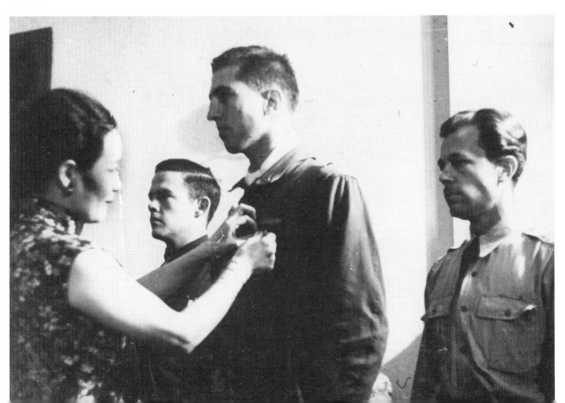

Above: Madame Chiang Kai-shek speaks after investing the Doolittle Raiders on 29 June 1942. One source states that she is reading the citation. Doolittle is standing second from the right, with, to his left, Major John Hilger. The Chinese official holding the paper has not been identified. (NARA)

Opposite page: A large crowd of Chinese has gathered to say farewell to some of Doolittle's men before they begin their journey home. (NARA)

Below: A small group of the survivors of the attack pose for the camera prior to their departure from China. (NARA)

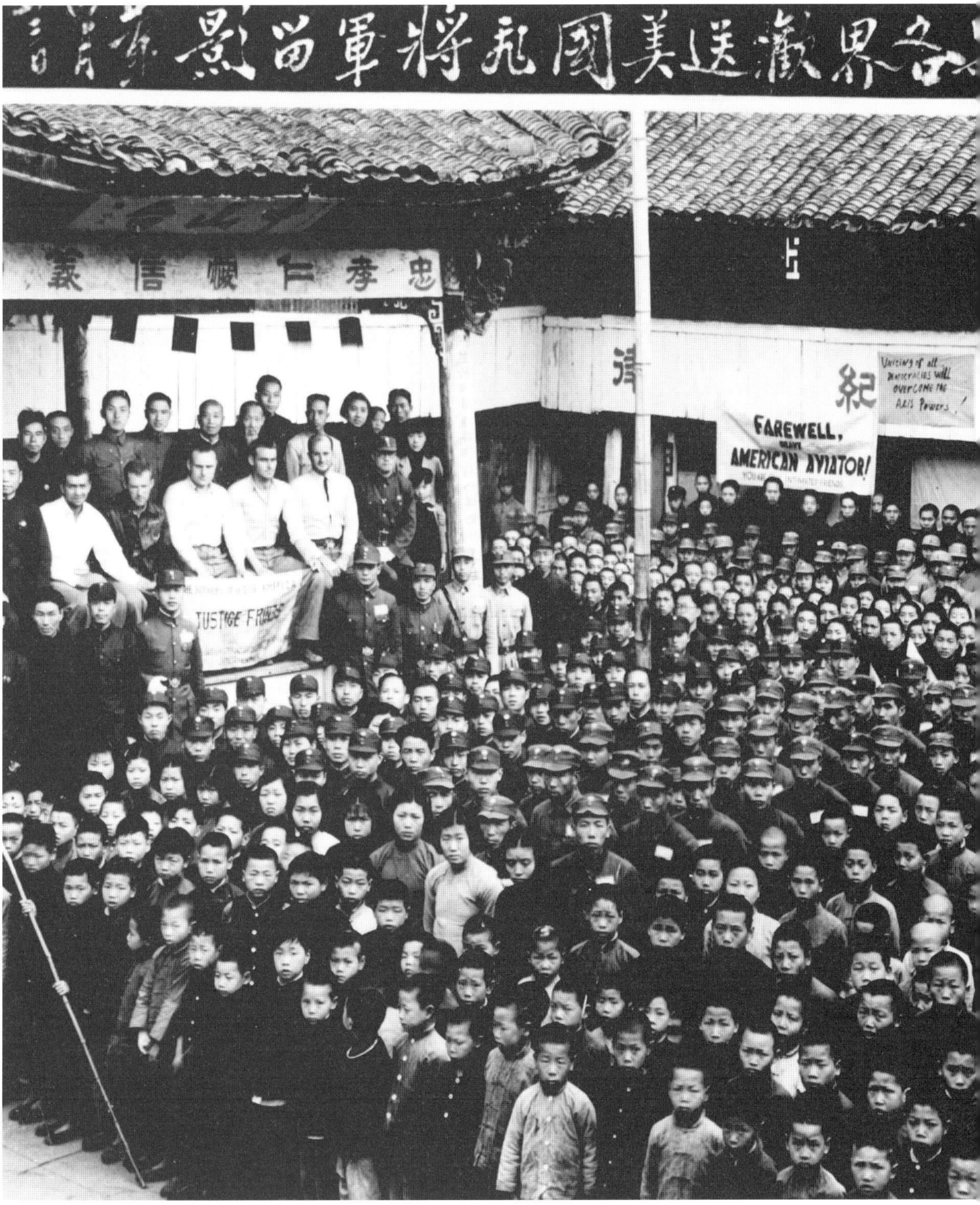
各界歡送美國飛將軍留影
忠孝仁愛信義
FAREWELL,
AMERICAN AVIATOR!

Above: Some of the survivors of the attack pictured beside a B-25, #41-12506 nicknamed *Obliterators Excuse Please*, at an airfield in China, 18 September 1942. (NARA)

Right: Brigadier General James H. Doolittle points to Tokyo on a globe sometime after his return to the United States following the Raid. (US Air Force)

Opposite page: Pictured during 1943, Brigadier General James H. Doolittle poses beside an Army Air Forces recruiting poster which makes reference to the April 1942 raid on Japan. (US Air Force)

148

Above: A group of officers and aircrew pictured after returning from a mission over enemy territory, 16 February 1943. They are: Major General James H. Doolittle; Lieutenant Colonel Anthony G. Hunter; Lieutenant Colonel F.H. Hills, Base Commander; Lieutenant Colonel H.H. Hinman; Major Bell, Executive Officer of Bombardment Group; Major G.E. Hall, Commander of a Bombardment Squadron; and Captain Moore, the General's aide. (US National Museum of the US Navy)

Opposite page: Doolittle receives the Army Distinguished Service Medal from General Dwight D. Eisenhower at a ceremony in North Africa. Announced in the War Department's General Orders No.49 (1943), it was awarded 'for exceptionally meritorious and distinguished services to the Government of the United States, in a duty of great responsibility as Commander of the Northwest African Strategic Air Force since its organization. Under his guidance and direction, this Force has developed a high degree of efficiency and accuracy and brought about, in great measure, a critical reduction in the supplies and reinforcements needed by the enemy. General Doolittle's energy, good judgment, exceptional qualities of leadership and wholehearted cooperation were primary factors in the ultimate success of air operations during the Tunisian Campaign.' (US National Museum of the US Navy)

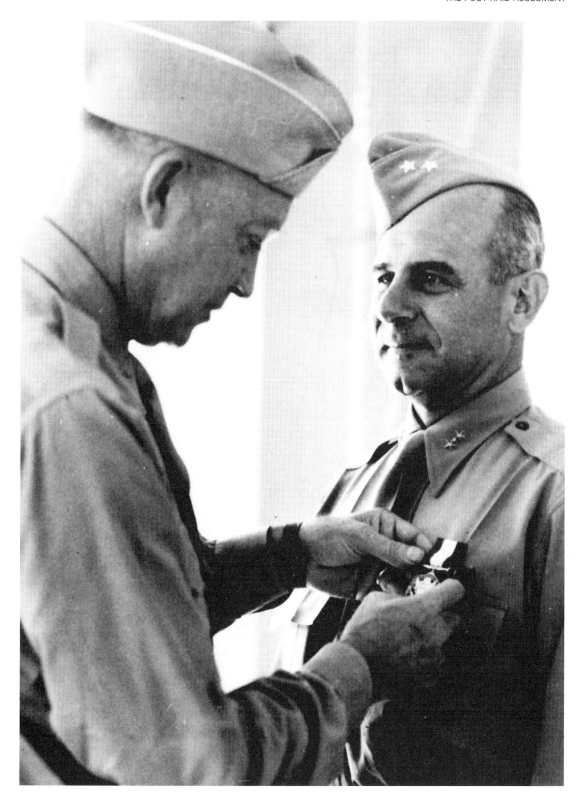

Above: Doolittle and some of the Raiders raise a salute during an anniversary dinner held in a North African farmhouse on 18 April 1943. All of the men in this gathering had participated in the raid itself or in the preparation for it. (NARA)

Opposite page top: The Essex-class aircraft carrier USS *Shangri-La* (CV-38) is christened by Mrs. James H. Doolittle at the Norfolk Navy Yard, Virginia, on 24 February 1944. The naming of this ship represented a radical departure from the general convention then adopted by the US Navy, which was to name aircraft carriers after battles or previous American ships. This break with tradition was the result of the Doolittle Raid, after which President Roosevelt was asked by reporters where the attack had originated from. He replied, 'They came from our secret base at Shangri-La', the fictional place described in the 1933 novel *Lost Horizon* by the British author James Hilton. (USNHHC)

Opposite page bottom: Mrs. James H. Doolittle, in the centre holding the flowers, pictured during the naming ceremony for USS *Shangri-La* on 24 February 1944. (US National Museum of the US Navy)

Right: At an airfield 'somewhere in Britain', General Spaatz (second from left) and Lieutenant General Doolittle (third from left) discuss results of a bombing attack with Eighth Air Force aircrew who just returned from the mission. (NARA)

Above: Between January 1944 and September 1945, Doolittle held his largest command, the Eighth Air Force, then based in Britain, as a lieutenant general, his promotion date being 13 March 1944.

Above: Some of the surviving Raiders pictured at one of their reunions, in this case the one that was held at Miami Beach between 18 and 21 April 1947. Doolittle himself is seated in the centre, with his right arm around Charles Greening, his left around John Hilger. The men in the front row, left to right, are: Waldo Bither; Richard Joyce; J. Royden Stork; Richard Knobloch; Thadd Blanton; unknown; and William Bower. (NARA)

Right: Lieutenant General Doolittle pictured whilst commanding the Eighth Air Force. His promotion to lieutenant general represented the highest rank ever held by an active US reserve officer in modern times. (US Department of Defense)

Above: On 4 April 1985, the US Congress advanced Doolittle to full general on the Air Force retired list. In a ceremony six days later, President Reagan and Senator Goldwater pinned on his four-star insignia, making him the first person in Air Force Reserve history to wear four stars. (White House Press Office)

Right: A portrait of General James H. Doolittle taken on 2 May 1986. Doolittle retired from USAF duty on 28 February 1959. (US Department of Defense)

Top Left: One of the Doolittle Raiders, Lieutenant Colonel Dick Cole, shakes hands with Robert Cressman, a historian at the US Navy's History and Heritage Command, at a luncheon held at the Army Navy Club in Washington, D.C. on 7 November 2014. At the time of the event, Cole was one of only four surviving members of Doolittle's force, of whom just two attended the luncheon.

Cole recalled that that the part of the mission that he 'found the scariest' was the onward flight to China: 'We were on our instruments; it was night and we were at 9,000 feet. We hit the Chinese coast. At that time the gas gauges were beginning to get close to empty. The airplane, carrying the homing station we were supposed to use to land, had crashed on the way there. Once in a while we could see lights, but the Chinese thinking we were the Japanese, immediately closed off most of their lights. That was the scariest time, looking down at that black hole and not knowing where you were or how you were going to land.' (US Navy)

Top right: The second Doolittle veteran to attend the event in Washington D.C. on 7 November 2014, was Lieutenant Colonel Ed Saylor, a member of Lieutenant Smith' crew No.15. During the luncheon, Rich Cole, Dick Cole's son, recounted a story concerning Saylor's time on US *Hornet*. One of the engines on #40-2267 was malfunctioning, and if it was unable to be repaired, the bomber would have to be pushed over the edge of the carrier's flight deck.

'Saylor decided he was going to take the engine off the aircraft, fix it and put it back on,' Rich Cole told the audience. 'They were in forty-foot swells and anything you put on the deck was going to go over the side. He and the Navy guys that were helping him took the engine off and took it below, disassembling it completely. The Navy folks in the machine shop fixed the sprocket that was acting up. Saylor put it back together and put it on the aircraft. When he was asked whether he thought it would work, he uttered a phrase I don't think any man has ever uttered in the history of the world. "Well, there weren't any parts left over."' (US Navy)

Above: During a ceremony on 19 September 2016, the USAF's new long-range stealth strategic bomber, the secretive Northrop Grumman B-21, was officially named the 'Raider' in honour of the men who had attacked Japan on 18 April 1942. The announcement was made by the then sole surviving member of Doolittle's force, Lieutenant Colonel Richard Cole – seen here during the ceremony with Technical Sergeant Derek White, assigned to the Maryland Air National Guard, and Air Force Secretary Deborah Lee James. (US Air Force/Scott M. Ash)

Left: Lieutenant Colonel (Ret.) Richard E. Cole toasts the fallen Raiders in a private ceremony at the National Museum of the U.S. Air Force on 18 April 2017. (US Air Force)

CHAPTER 6

Recreating History

21 April 1992

Above: As part of the preparations for the 1992 re-enactment, the volunteer crews of the B-25s were put through a series of training exercises. Here, Lieutenant Greg Sullivan USN, the catapult officer from the aircraft carrier USS *Ranger*, practises a deck 'launch' with the crew of B-25 #44-30748, nicknamed *Heavenly Body*, on land at Naval Air Station North Island. (NARA)

'The American B-25 Mitchell bombers revved up on the carrier deck. As their crews conducted pre-flight checks, they were too busy to consider the risks. On the bridge, Quartermaster 2nd Class Carl Nelson turned the carrier into the wind.

'Aware of the mission's historical importance, photographer Bill Gibson intently filmed the action. The distinctive sound of the B-25 held everyone's attention. The Navy flight officer signaled the launch was a go. Awkwardly beautiful with its 67.5-foot wingspan, the plane steadily headed toward the bow. The B-25 was airborne! A few minutes later, another roared into the morning sky.'

This account was published in the July 1992 issue of *All Hands*, the magazine of the US Navy. It was not, however, referring to the historic events of 18 April 1942, but an almost as remarkable achievement performed some fifty years later to mark the 50th anniversary of the Doolittle Raid.

As a twenty-three-year-old Quartermaster 2nd Class, Carl Nelson had been the helmsman on USS *Hornet* on the day that Doolittle's raiders launched their attack. Likewise, at the time Bill Gibson was serving as a Photographer's Mate Second Class on *Hornet*, his role being to record for posterity, and of course publicity, the mission's preparations and departure. Indeed, some of the pictures on the previous pages may well have been his work.

Remarkably, the Doolittle Raid was not the last time that a B-25 was flown of the deck of a US Navy aircraft carrier. On Tuesday, 21 April 1992, almost fifty years to the day since the raiders' strike against Japan, a pair of veteran B-25 Mitchells was launched from the deck of the *Forrestal*-class supercarrier USS *Ranger* (CV-61) as part of the commemorations of the attack. For the occasion, both Nelson and Gibson agreed to return to their wartime roles. They were not the only ones, for also present on *Ranger* were three of the surviving Raiders and a Chinese interpreter who had guided many of the downed crewmen to safety.

USS *Ranger* was at sea off San Diego when, for the second time in his life, Carl Nelson stood at the helm of a US Navy aircraft carrier which was about to launch B-25 bombers. Captain Dennis McGinn, *Ranger*'s commanding officer, had been more than happy to let Nelson repeat his role for the historic event. 'Fifty years later, Warrant Officer Nelson hasn't lost his touch,' McGinn later confirmed.

Speaking to the press on *Ranger*, Nelson recalled the launch in 1942: 'Our speed was about 25 knots and I think the wind was about the same. That gave us about 50 knots of wind across the deck, which the pilots needed because it was a short take-off. We didn't really know how important the raid was going to be … The captain [Captain Marc A. Mitscher] had asked the navigator to make sure I had the wheel for the launch because I knew how to steer the ship real well.'[26]

For his part in the anniversary event, Bill Gibson recreated his original role by shooting film footage of the B-25s taking-off for a documentary.

The event had been inspired by Bradly Grose, who had first proposed the idea of the re-enactment in 1989. At the time, Grose was a director of the Eagle Field Museum, which was located on the site of a Second World War training airfield in Southern California. With the assistance of Task Force 16 veteran Vice-Admiral William Houser Retd., the suggestion was approved by the Pentagon in January 1992. At that point, the US Pacific Fleet, which was stationed at Naval Air Station North Island in San Diego Bay, was handed the assignment. There was just three months to plan and execute this new mission.

The results, as the images included here testify, was a resounding success. Pilot Steve Crow was the first to take-off in *Heavenly Body*. Following behind was pilot William Klaers at the controls of *In the Mood*. The two B-25s circled the carrier as they formed up with five other B-25s in three elements for a 'missing man' formation. The other five B-25s flying in the formation were *Pacific Princess*, *Executive Sweet*, *Mitch the Witch*, *Tootsie*, and *Axis Nightmare*.[27]

It had been hoped that General Doolittle himself would have been present on *Ranger* as guest of honour. Unfortunately, circumstances decided otherwise, and he was duly represented by his grandson, Peter Doolittle. A quality engineer in the aerospace industry, Peter read out the following apology: 'Unfortunately, at 95 I am no longer able to travel and regret not being able to be with you and the fine men and women of the Pacific Fleet.'

Since Doolittle could not participate, a small squadron of historic B-25 Mitchells and P-51 Mustangs flew 500 miles north to his home on the Monterey Peninsula, which is part of the central California coast. There they dipped their wings in salute, before releasing a cascade of red, white and blue carnations into the waters of the Pacific. Understandably moved by this aerial tribute, Doolittle gazed skyward as the aircraft thundered overhead.

Opposite page top: *Heavenly Body* at the quayside at Naval Air Station North Island, with USS *Ranger* in the background. (NARA)

Opposite page bottom: The moment that *Heavenly Body* is swung aboard the carrier by the crane. (NARA)

Below: *Heavenly Body* pictured being towed to a pier at Naval Air Station North Island, from where it will be lifted by crane aboard USS *Ranger*. (NARA)

Above: *Heavenly Body* pictured safely parked on USS *Ranger*'s flight deck. Delivered from the factory on 20 February 1945, *Heavenly Body* was immediately declared war surplus and placed in storage. (NARA)

Opposite page: A view of *Heavenly Body*'s nose section prior to her take-off from USS *Ranger*. With a flight deck some 1,000-feet long, *Ranger* provided *Heavenly Body*'s crew a longer take-off, by some 200-odd feet, over that afforded Doolittle's force whilst operating from *Hornet*. (US Navy/Journalist 1st Class Joe Gawlowicz)

Left: One of *Heavenly Body*'s crew for the commemorative take-off, Ed Gustafson, pictured wearing a vintage Army Air Corps uniform, describes the take-off to some spectators on US *Ranger* on 21 April 1992. (NARA)

Left: The two B-25s that participated in the 50th anniversary carrier launching are pictured parked on the rear of the flight deck of USS *Ranger* whilst the carrier was underway in the Pacific in April 1992. (NARA)

Above: One of the crew members of *In the Mood* cleans the nose windows prior to her take-off. Delivered on 1 September 1944, #44-29199 was never allocated to an operational bomber unit and only served in various training roles. (NARA)

Above: Some of *Ranger*'s flight deck personnel in action as *Heavenly Body*'s engines are warmed up in preparation for her launch. Two other B-25s, #44-30801 *Executive Suite* and #43-28204 *Pacific Princess* (the oldest of the four), had been on standby at NAS North Island but, in the event, were not required. (NARA)

Opposite page top: A close-up of the two B-25s on *Ranger*'s flight deck. In front is *Heavenly Body*, with, behind, #44-29199 which was named *In the Mood*. Now residing at the US National Museum of World War II Aviation, *In the Mood* also has the distinction of being launched off USS *Carl Vinson* twice in 1995. (NARA)

Opposite page bottom: *Heavenly Body* is waved off to begin her run down USS *Ranger*'s flight deck. She was the first of the two B-25s to get airborne on 21 April 1992. (NARA)

Main Image: History is made as, mirroring the events of 18 April 1942, *Heavenly Body* takes off from USS *Ranger*. Over 1,500 guests were embarked to witness the event. (US Navy/Journalist 1st Class Joe Gawlowicz)

Above: *Heavenly Body* slowly gains altitude as she passes down the carrier's flight deck. (NARA)

Right: Moments after *Heavenly Body* had taken-off, it was *In the Mood*'s turn to get airborne. Note the large crowd in the background. (NARA)

Main Image: *In the Mood* heads off to join *Heavenly Body* and the other waiting B-25s to create the 'missing man' formation.

REFERENCES AND NOTES

1. Patrick Clancey, *Halsey-Doolittle Raid, April 1942*, on the Hyper War Foundation website.
2. Lieutenant Commander J.H. Doolittle, *Report on Japanese Raid, Military Intelligence*, pp.5-6.
3. Information drawn from the Headquarters of the Army Air Forces' report of 9 July 1942, entitled *General Doolittle's Report on Japanese Raid, April 18, 1942*.
4. Colonel Charles R. Greening, *The First Joint Action, A Historical Account of the Doolittle Tokyo Raid – April 18, 1942*, on www.doolittleraider.com.
5. Mary Claire Kendall, 'Doolittle's Raiders and the Miracle That Saved Them', www.forbes.com.
6. Quoted on: www.doolittleraider.com/interviews.htm.
7. Carroll V. Glines, *Doolittle's Tokyo Raiders* (Van Nostrand Reinhold, London, 1981), p.164.
8. Duane Schultz, *The Doolittle Raid* (St. Martin's Press, New York, 1988), pp.195-6.
9. Quoted on: www.barrybradford.com/guest-post-lieutenant-dean-e-hallmark-the-doolittle-raiders.
10. ibid.
11. Richard Goldstein, 'David Thatcher, Part of '42 Doolittle Raid on Japan, Dies at 94', *The New York Times*, 22 June 2016.
12. See www.warfarehistorynetwork.com/daily/wwii/the-unsolved-mysteries-of-the-doolittle-raid.
13. Quoted on www.workersforjesus.com/tgriffin.htm.
14. Schultz, p.166.
15. For more information, please see: childrenofthedoolittleraiders.com.
16. This description is based on that given by John Chandler Griffin in *Lt. Bill Farrow, Doolittle Raider* (Pelican, Gretna, 2007), pp.155-162.
17. See, Duane Schultz, pp.232-3.
18. For more information, see Case No.25 of the United States Military Commission, Shanghai, 27 February to 15 April 1946.
19. Quoted in *Osprey's Battles of World War II, Japan 1942, America's First Strike Back at Japan* (Osprey, Botley, 2006), p.83.
20. Glines, p.383.
21. ibid, p.384.
22. Quoted in James M. Scott, *Target Tokyo, Jimmy Doolittle and the Raid that Avenged Pearl Harbor* (Norton, London, 2015), p.321.
23. Schultz, p.252.
24. See www.smithsonianmag.com/history/untold-story-vengeful-japanese-attack-doolittle-raid.
25. Craig Nelson, *The First Heroes, The Extraordinary Story of the Doolittle Raid – America's First World War II Victory* (Corgi, London, 2002), pp.319-20.
26. Quoted on *The Sextant*, https://usnhistory.navylive.dodlive.mil.
27. For more information, please see www.b-25history.org.